MOGWIE-IDAN
Stories of the land

LIONEL GEORGE FOGARTY

MOGWIE-IDAN
Stories of the land

Co-edited by Ali Cobby Eckermann
with an introduction by Ali Alizadeh

Vagabond Press | Indigenous Australian Writing

Acknowledgments: Some of these poems have previously appeared in *The Best Australian Poems 2010* (Black Inc, 2010), *Connection Requital* (Vagabond Press, 2010), *Kudjela* (Private printing, 1983), *Southerly*, *Yerrabilela Jimbelung* (Keeaira Press, 2004). A special thank you to Anne Josefine Botz (Germany) and Aurelie Pouget (France) for their friendship with this project.

First published by Vagabond Press. First edition, 2012.
Transnational edition, 2015.
PO Box 958 Newtown NSW 2042 Australia
www.vagabondpress.net

Designed and typeset by Michael Brennan
in Minion Pro 11/14

ISBN 978-1-922181-64-0

This book is dedicated to my son Jabreeni

and to my grandchildren
Nyariah, Munjindi and Dangula
Wudarabin, Ilyaree, Violet, Marika and Nyurin
Guyahny, Gulwa, Gulbari, Geoffrey and Goothala
Jarvelin, Jalahny, Yalburu, Wongarah, Kaialgoom
Djahn and Gulka

and to all my other family kinship grandchildrens

Jingi Whallo

Hello how are you all?

Nunyan Nyarri Lionel

My name is Lionel

Gita Gita Yoondoo Jarjum

Good morning you children

Yuway Yoojum Dhagun

Yo Yoogum Yoogum Balugalun

Kanungin Whallo

We pay our respects to the … people and spirits of this area.

I come from Yugambeh Yuggera and Kutjela people and I am proud to acknowledge the custodians, the traditional people the …

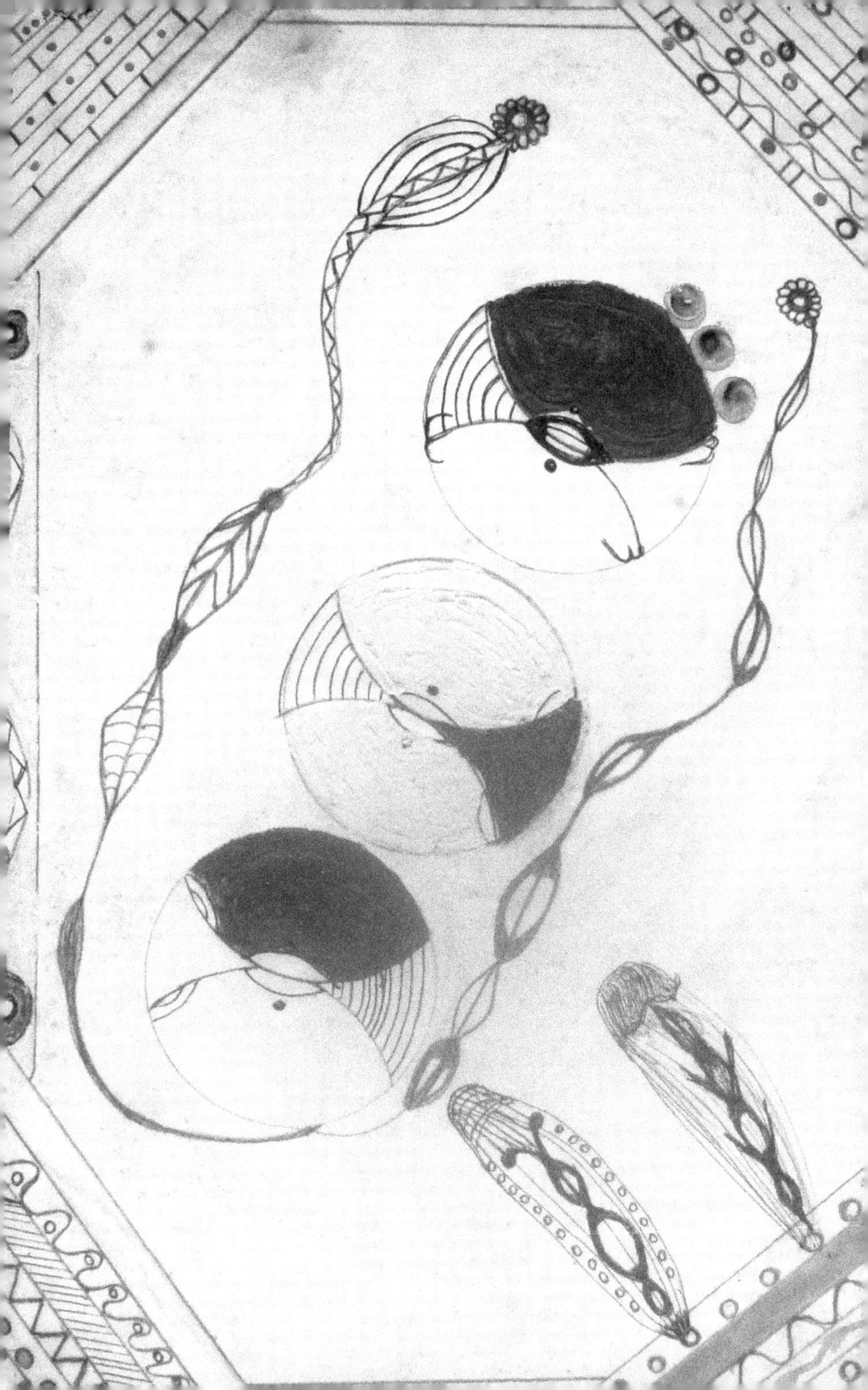

CONTENTS

Introduction

How does one think and write about the extraordinary poetry of Lionel Fogarty and his superb new book, *Mogwie-Idan: Stories of the Land*?

In a literary environment saturated with hyperbolic praise and prize money heaped upon young mediocrities and their older, overrated mentors and benefactors, how does one approach the work of a poet as brazenly singular, as unapologetically radical as Australia's foremost *guerrilla poet*? And in a capitalist society where poetry is forced to exist culturally as either commercial entertainment – *spoken word*, *slam poetry* and so on – or as a fetish object to mark status, bourgeois sophistry and sham cosmopolitanism, how can one begin to talk about a poet whose work entails nothing short of a perpetual revolution and transformation of the very substance of poetry?

To say that Fogarty's poetry exists outside and beyond the aesthetic regimes of contemporary Australian poetry would be an understatement. The poems in this collection are unlike anything else being currently written, and they are almost incomprehensible under the rubrics used for appreciating and discussing most contemporary poetry. His is neither the superficial, playful experimentalism cherished by the proponents of popular culture and postmodernism, nor the facile, sentimental evocation of place and landscape that conservative aesthetes expect of Indigenous artists.

Fogarty's is a combative political poetry too complex and innovative to be labelled didactic, and a profoundly inventive and unconventional voice that can't be reduced to mere formal idiosyncrasy. This provocatively paradoxical symbiosis of political commitment and stylistic improbability can be exemplified in the following lines from the poem 'Receiver,' as included in this collection, a lively conflation of Marxian terminology, profanity and spoken language.

> Waging roving counter revolutionary
> Are them Blackfellas in capitalist minds
> A single spark can bit you two half and
> A single bourgeois idealist can fuckup
>
> Betrayed economic fragile social buggered structure

One approach over the last two decades has been to view Fogarty's unique work as the application of a postcolonial poetics, as the most vivid illustration of a creolised aesthetics in contemporary Australian literature. This view could account for the heady fusion and collision of Aboriginal words and motifs with English phrases and English grammar in much of Fogarty's work; yet I feel such a perspective runs the risk of reducing Fogarty's poetry to a rather simplistic reflection of Aboriginality, and it understates the palpably revolutionary dynamics of his work.

There is no doubt that the poems in *Mogwie-Idan: Stories of the Land*, perhaps more so than some of Fogarty's other collections, include a deep affection for his people's unique social and spiritual notions, but they remain too linguistically mischievous and conceptually challenging to be seen as celebrations of a cultural milieu or the articulations of an ethnic condition. It is difficult to see, for example, the following lines from the poem 'Blurb Critics,' as a direct expression of their author's Murri identity.

There the Murri carnivorous shadow
Port trampoline tenor activates
mad guess validation came
looking for self-interrogative

Poetry like this rejects both interpretation as well as conservative aesthetic apperception in the same stroke. But the syntactic formation of 'carnivorous shadow' madly 'looking for self-interrogative' has a depth and gravity that can't be constrained under the signs of self-reflexivity and indeterminacy. Even if it's clear that Fogarty's poem is not interested in directly signifying a reality, it is also clear that his text is undeniably haunted by the powerful force of an ineffable Real.

Consider these lines from the wonderful poem, 'Burgeon Assemble Energy':

Beyond naked air an unmade
body thunders a nymph
aboard space ductile
humble dark winged-veined mothers.

You'll fear Dad's father's
unborn groans verging pressure
off lights deaths in search of you

One may note the poem's allusions to the Dreamtime, and its author's characteristically creative ungrammatical sentence structures and phrasing. But these attributes alone do not account for the poem's power. Whatever exists 'beyond naked air', that is, beyond the entirely visible yet empty space of the present, beyond what we breathe and cannot transcend or break with, is the shattering Void of 'an unmade body thunder'.

This is not a poetics of surrealism or absurdity but one of an inexistent truth rupturing the state of existing knowledge. The 'nymphs' that emerge from the unmaking of the body culminate, with the primordial yet unnatural resonances of 'dark winged-veined mothers', into something 'you'll fear', into a Name of the Father – 'father's unborn groans'. Air has vanished in the images of nymphs and winged mothers, but these symbolic images are themselves cancelled by the terror of patriarchal 'pressure', and foreclosed in the permanence of 'deaths in search of you.'

What is already conceivable and known is that death is a physical event, and that, depending on one's beliefs, there may or may not exist a personal spirit which may or may not enjoy an afterlife. Fogarty's poem breaks with this knowledge, and by so doing introduces a radically new thought that is both entirely embodied within the poem and is absolutely unique to the poem. He gives us, in other words, *a truth* in the form of a deeply unthinkable proposal on *immortal mortality*: the 'deaths' are non-physical and celestial – they come from 'beyond naked air' – and they have no interest in the 'unmade' body, but neither are they intangible, hallucinatory apparitions; you the reader shall hear and fear their 'groans' as they are and forever will be 'in search of you.'

To draw on the ideas of the radical French thinker Alain Badiou, the truth of this poetry is *immanent* – that is, it is situated within the poem itself and is proven by the operations of the poem – and also *singular*. In other words, what Fogarty's poetry tells us can only be told in a poem. To use Badiou's phrase, Fogarty's poetry is a *truth-procedure*, and, in my view, his is one of the only poetries in contemporary Australian writing that can be adequately described as such. It is therefore imperative to read and study the work of Lionel Fogarty if Australian poetry is to be more than a field of triviality and rivalry between and amongst careerist upstarts and grudge-infested gatekeepers. I agree entirely with John Kinsella that Fogarty is 'the most vital poet writing in Australia today' (11).

Ali Alizadeh

Work Cited

Kinsella, J. Introduction. *The Penguin Anthology of Australian Poetry.* Camberwell: Penguin, 2009.

LIST OF ILLUSTRATIONS

P.2	Mia mia (Home)
P.7	Burrima (Fire man)
P.12	Hand off duwa (You can't take my Spirit)
P.38	Barang dumburra (Coming in full circuit)
P.50	Tundera breast (Thunder)
P.55	Buya (Pull)
P.59	Toggul (Pumping of heart)
P.64	Gauwal (Far away)
P.92	Bube (Clouds)
P.96	Minyungai (When, what time)
P.111	Dhalumbirale (Fish with a hook)
P.114	Moocoo (The emu womb)
P. 120	Gurara (Large)
P. 121	Gilli gilli (Get away from me)
P. 145	Dha dhagun (Earth 2)
P. 150	Quinama (Told man rainbow man)
P. 152	Gulwa (Koala)
P. 153	Dha dhagun (Earth 1)

CONNECTION REQUITAL

BURN THE BRIDGES

YOU ARE VULNERABLE AS GLASS ARE FALL TO PEACES
WHEN TOILED OF THE STRIPPING OF OUR PRIDES

YOU ARE RESTLESS IN LIFE
WHEN WE'VE BORN ANOTHER TO FIGHT

ALL THE BRIDGES OF YOUR MUSIC WILL BURN AS SOON
AS YOU WALK TO THE CENTRE OF OUR PROBLEMS

YOU MIGHT HAVE MOVED TO OUR SACRED RIGHTS
BUT YOUR PRICE IS HIGH IN

INTEREST RATES AND THEN YOU PROWL AROUND
UNRESPECTFUL TO ALL BLACK FAMILYS HOMES

YOU ARE THEY DAT WATCH PROTECT AND
LAUGH AS THE BLACKFELLAS RISE

THE WAITING FOR THE SUNRISE IS LIKE WAITING FOR A PAST
OF PEOPLE TO COME AND PROCLAIM THE LAND

BUT SITTING HERE BLOCKING OUT THE UNJUSTIFIABLE SINS
SINS ARE WHAT YOU ARE DOING

PARADOX HEARING

MIMICKING THE LIGHTS BETWEEN MISTY MOONLIGHTING
TROPICAL NIGHTS MEET MORNINGS UNENDING DROUGHT
OUR NATIVES FERTILE THE SANDS
DAT MASKED LOVE TO MASSACRED ROCKS
THOSE ANCESTORS WERE NOT MINE

YET WHITE EXPLORERS CAME TO IMAGE
GIVEN ACROSS TODAYS GROOVED LANGUAGE
MIMIC THE SOFT SINGING PASSED DOWN FROM OUR UNIVERSE
MUMMA GLISTEN HER LIPS RED SPEAKING
MUMMA GRASSED HER BODY YELLOW REACHING

OUR NATIVES SLEPT WHEN DEBRIS
FALLEN HOURS NOW WE STAND RIBCAGED
CELL PITCH BRIGHTNESS BLACKER MORNINGS
BUT BACK AT THE TROPICAL NIGHTS
TREMBLE SEEM NOT IN OUR SPIRITS

A RUMBLE FUTURE RANG OUT A MESSAGE
ETERNITY RESOUNDS YOUR ANCIENT RHYTHM
THE PARADOX WAVES OF PEOPLE EVAPORATED
LIFE RELINQUISHED TO TENDER EVENINGS
THE TELEVISION HEAPED COASTAL DELIGHTS

YET WE X=DESTRUCTIONED HERITAGE LINKING
WATER TO SNAKES ON EARTH PLANTS
YET WE SUPPLY ROOTS AMONG THEIR MIDST
DESPERATION BECAME A GREED YOU NOW TAKE
FOR 'PETER'S SAKE' YOU DIDN'T WALK ON THE MOON MAN
HEY PRECIOUS FAUNA ERADICATE MANY
PLAGUES OF DIMINISHING HUMAN POISONS

MIMICKING OUR POETRY OR RECITING HIT

I WON'T GLOW DARK GREEN ORANGE PURPLE
YES JUST TO PINK OUR CONDOLENCES AT TONGUES

AUTUMN SUMMER WINTER RAINBOWFUL GOT SCORNED
OUR NATIVES FERTILE THE SAND
DAT MADE LOVE TO MASSACRED ROCK
MIMICKING THE LIGHT OF GOODNESS ABO ABO'S ABO'S

KILL THE OPPRESSOR BLACK WRITERS
AS BLACK WRITERS WE MUST CAUSE PRESSURES
TO THE BLACKS TO GET UP AND FIRE THE WHITE EDITORS
AND WHITE PUBLISHING HOUSE DOWN TO THE GROUNDS
WHERE WE TAKE AND BURN THE MARKET PLACES

TO A UNFAMILIAR EXCHANGEABLE

**DEDICATED TO 4 000 AUST INDIGENOUS AUTHORS*

DREAMS

WHERE THERE IS NATURE
THERE MUST BE REAL DREAMS
WE KNOW DREAMS

WE KNOW DREAMS COME OUT OF FIRST YOUR OWN
AND CAN GET OUT OF BRAIN AND WANDER ON
THE SURF OF A TURF WHERE BADDEST BLOODS AROSE

LONG THE WAIT FOR DREAMING
THE MORE TESTS LIVES GET CAUGHT
AT TIMELESS WARP

LONG SMALL IN BETWEEN DREAMS DON'T
HAVE TO BE IN A DEEP SLEEP OR FAST SLEEP
YO IT'S IN THE BACK HEART; BACK SPIRITUAL;

BACK LAND; BACK RIVERS; BLACK ROCK
TRAGEDY TOWARDS TRAGEDY
TOWARDS A BRACKEN STUMBLING AND SCREAMING

ALARM TOWARDS THE PLAINS

TOKEN BLINDFOLDED ADVISORY ABORIGINAL COUNCIL ZIG ZAGS NEWS WE BLAME YOUSE

TO PAINT ABOUT TODAY 'IN ABORIGINAL WAYS'
MUST FIND VERY HARD TO ART THE TACK
CONNING DOWN OUTBACK ARTISTS
THEN TOLD GET OUT OF ARTIST SURROUNDS
WELL A PAINT GOT TO BE DANCED
  GOT TO BE PROVED
  GOT TO BE REVOLUTION
BEAUTY AND LIVE AND LINE
TO EVEN SIT ON THE GROUND IS DANCING
WITH OUR SPIRITS
TO LEAVE BEHIND A SHONE MOON
AND NOT CONJURE THE ACTION
TO THE PLACE OR FALLEN LOVE
SADNESS IS SOMETHING ALL FELT
THINGS UNDER SAME RAIL
ROCK TREE DIRT SAND WATER
WE ARE YOUR BROTHERS AND SISTERS
SOCIETY OF NO CARING WE ARE
NOT IN NEED OF YOUR HURTS
PAIN COMES IN MANY AND CUTS ACROSS ALL RACES
AND IF AN ORIGIN IS TOLD
NOT TO BE FORCED IT'S OLD
PAINT US THEN SPEAR
BOOMERANG WARRIOR SHIELD CLAPSTICK
A VOICE HEART BEAT TO THOSE FORGOTTEN ARTISTS
PROJECT REALISATION NEUTRAL INVASION
HAPPEN EVERY WHICH WAY; HERE AT PRESENT
AREAS ARE LEGISLATIVE LEGS FOR A RUN
BY PROVING OUR GATHERING AS THAT
WE DO SOCIAL DYING
LIVES ALIVE

2.

NATIONAL TOPICS ARE NOT HARD ARTS
PITJANJATJARA BE US
PITJANJATJARA ME FELLA GAS BILLS
BY SYSTEM MINING
REALITY SOUTH
BOTH FARMERS ARE PURCHASED
IN CHASING ENVIRONMENTAL
BE US THREATENED
HIM I DON'T TAKE
YET HE MOVES LATE WITH PASTORAL ACT
SHE HANDS MINISTER FOUNDATION
THAT WE IS REAL ESTATE WITHOUT PAPERS
OUR COUNCILS LOBBY DESERTS
CAUSE 'HARMONEY' GOT WINDED
VOTING WAS NOW ALL FOR NOBODY
THIS SEEMED GOOD TO PITJANJATJARA
PASSAGES OF SOIL
STEPPED OVER RELATING LEGS
TWELVE MONTHS OVERGRAZING
HOUSES TURNED PARLIAMENT
THEN RABBITS CLAWED
ALIEN RULES LANGUAGED BEHAVOUR
HISTORICAL
LIKE WHAT YA WHITFELLA VICTIM US
DRAFT ASSISTING DEMANDS
WHEN OUTSTATION ALREADY THERE
PITJANTAJARA RETREATS
WHAT EXECUTIVE VALUE WANTS
WHEN WE SELL GUT HEART BRAIN TONGUES
FOR YOUSE SO
COME ON DOWN
AND FREEHOLD US

3.

ABO'S THAT ARE IN THE PIT OF ASSAULTING JARS
MY PITJANTAJARA CRY
A SAD MELTING LAND RIGHTS
COPE NO MORE
DON'T DO IT.
THE FIGHT STILL CRYS
  CRY FOR YOUSE
I DON'T HATE WHITE PEOPLE
I DON'T SAVE BLACK PEOPLE
I WON'T HELP KILL YOU
STRANGLED OPPRESSED RUSHING AFRAIDNESS
  FOR YOUSE
BUT PURSUE FREEDOM I DO
BUT KILL INDUSTRY RACIST I DO
JUSTIFY TO YOU I WON'T DO
  FUCK YOU
PLANNED OPPORTUNISM I WILL DO
SHIT; AGREE WE HUMAN
WISH I'M UNITY WITH YOU
MUST BE REALNESS
I DON'T LOVE YOUR DAUGHTER FOR FUN
I DON'T SADDEN YOUR FEELINGS FOR FUN
I WON'T LIVE WAYS YOU GIVE
KNOWING IT CEASES WHEN YOU WANT IT TO
I WON'T LAY MY MIND TO BE PICKED
I WILL FORM MY BODY FRESH
I WILL LOVE YOUR CHILDREN
BUT FUCK ME WHEN I SAVE YOU
SOMETIMES THAT'S ALL I DO
ALL I HATE IS JUST SOCIETY
EVEN IF IT IS MADE UP OF WHITE
  WHAT IS FREEDOM
  WHAT IS HELPING

WHAT IS HUMAN FEELING
I SURE KNOW; CAUSE I LOVE ALL
I SURE FIND BONES
LIFE SAME SO WE APPRECIATE
SAVE; HELP; HATE FOR BADNESS
IN HUMANNESS
'DESTINY TO A MURRI CAME DISTRAUGHTING'
NURSERY RHYME GAVE LOT OF LOTS
MURRIS EAR HURTS
TWINKLING SHADOWS = BLAZING PAST PASSED
BODY HANGING
OUTLIVES TREE

INTRICACIES

INTRICACIES CAN
BE UNDERSTOOD
I KNOW YOU
I BELIEVE YOU
WHAT YOU THINK
BUT I AM NOT SURE
YOU REALISE
DAT WHAT YOU HEARD
IS NOT WHAT
I MEANT.

THE FERTILITY
IN ANY NEGATIVE
TABOO PERSONS
CLAIMING FABRICATED
INTRICATE FUNDAMENTAL
STRIKES OVER
SACRED SITES.

BUT IN YEARS TO COME
WILL PREVIOUSLY
NATIVE MURRIS
BE ACCEPTABLE
THE BELIEF TO A LIE
IS ONE AND
TWO HUNDREDS
IN A FUTURES.

DISASSOCIATE ITSELF

COUPS ARE INDEPENDENCE ON THE BEACH
COUPS ARE UNSUNG BATTLERS BREAKING FREE
COUPS ARE THOSE WHISPERING ARTS
FLEX ORIGINS NEVER DUNNY THE EBONY
WHEN CORRUGATION LOCUSTS THE CRUSTS
INCANDESCENCE SQUINTING ANNOUNCED SUMMERS
REFRACTED SEARCHLIGHT INCESSANT MAD HUMMING
PLUMAGE PRIMEVAL CHORUS GAVE UNIVERSALLY
ALL RAIDED DIVE GLEAMING SHRILL
WITHIN GARRULOUS WICKEDNESS STIFFENED AIR
BECAME SPRAY BUSTER SO ATROCIOUS
RAW YET IN SEWAGE
GENTRIFIED BY GLIMPSE IN HIGH PECULIARITY
FRAMED FRUITOLOGISTS
ENTIRE SWARMED BORDERLINE SLUMS TILED
SURPLUS SO CHEAP DAT DRAGGED
STAGGERED LACE OWL EYES SAW LOSERS
SELL LITTER SMASHED RUSTED PATIOS
COUPS IN SECTARIAN MIDGET HEDONISTIC
IN ALTERING OBSERVANCE EGO
COUPS OF RUBBER SANDALS APPEARED WHEN
RENOVATING BURNISHED THE MELANCHOLY
HOLY CRAGGY IMPOSED PLAGUE
WHERE RESPIRATORY SEEMS EXPECTED
COUPS COMPLETING LEAN VERSION BECOME
FATHERS AND ABLUTION BLOOD
EXORBITANT DEFIANCE REGARDING SACKS OF
STRIKE WOOED RADICALLY CONGLOMERATE
SUPERIOR CHAIN REACTION
MALNUTRITION IN THE GERRYMANDERING ARE HAPPENING
CAMPAIGNERS POVERTY TEAMS ANTI-PROGRAMME

BETRAYAL PROCEDURES DEAL VERY MUCH IN
RESERVES FOR THOSE BOUND TO LIFE DESTROYING LIFES
COOK AND DEM SAT WITH HIM DEEDS DEATH
EVIDENCE IN CATASTROPHE SHOWS TEARS OF
CHEEKS ROLLING OLIGARCHY
THE WORD BIGGER THAN THE DECAPITATION SOWN
FLEX EVENTS ARE PATCHING
COUPS UNDER SUPPRESS EMBARRASSMENTS
DISASSOCIATE ITSELF

MUTUAL FEVER

100 DEGREE TEMPERATURES IN NAKED HEAT WE CAN DO
DEATH CURSE BY UNTRIBAL MAN CAN'T
HOSPITALISE OUR PHYSICALITY
SHARES ACROSS THE VALLEY OF FLICKERING EYES
SAW CHILDBIRTHS BEFORE BIRTH
AND OUR LUBRA'S PASSIVELY GAVE TREMBLE
A WATERLESS SEA OF ASHES
FIREFLIES ROARED LIGHTS AROUND A SMALL BUSH
BLAZING CARCASSES MOANED TO BE DREAMT
PRE-DAWN STAGGERED WITH ONE MAN
WHO DRANK GLOBULES FLOODED WATERS PURE AHAHAH
YET; STRANGE INTERLOPERS OF KOOKABURRAS
SHRIEK A SHRIEK A CURIOSITY SCREAMING MELODYS
IMMEDIATELY BELOW CONSCIOUS OF A SONG
RIVULET BLACK MAN PULVERIZED ALL
HALF FORMED BODIES DANCING
BUT NEAR A OUTCROPPED FLOWER CAME A YELL
OF ANGUISHED MUSIC RIPE BUT RAW
COS ABILITY TO HOST ALMIGHTY FRONTIERS
STARES APPEALED THOSE TRAPPED BY THIS
UNTRIBAL MAN SINGING SONGS
IT WAS GETTING HOTTER AND COLDER THE TELLER TOLD
AND EXHAUSTION AT MORE JOURNEYS
SEEMED STARVATION TO FACING NEW BIRTH
AIR MINGLED A SPIRIT OF COLOURED LUNAR
CREATING LOOKS AT THOSE CARCASSES DREAMT
IN SILVER CRYSTAL GLASS LIKE COMIC BIZARRE DEATH TRIBAL MODERN
BUT BROTHERS AND SISTERS LIFE REFRACTED
A LIFEFUL SITE BY CAUTIOUSLY
SEEING DAT THIS IS OUR LANDNESS
ONE HUNDRED DEGREE TEMPERATURE WAS TRUE TO JAGG OUT
MONSTER MAN DIDN'T INSTINCTIVELY FEED MUTUAL FEVERS

EDITED FOR THE KEENS

CHEMICALS MADE OUR SEX
NATURE GAVE OUR RIGHTS
WITHOUT IMMUNE VESSELS
MAGGED BY BLOODS AND
RISKING KISSING
PREMATURE HARMLESS EXPOSES
ILLNESS CAN'T COME OFF LIFERS
SETTLED ON SEATS OF NO CELLS
THE BODY PURE MUST BE
THE LOST CAN'T LOWER
SHE AND HE WHO THEY ARE
AIR TO LIGHT ALWAYS A DARK
SIDE OF THE SUN
MOON ENTREE NIGHT
TO RAIN
ENCLOSURE DEEP IN INJURY STATED
JUSTICE SO SERIOUS; THE RESULTS
ARE POLLING NETTINGS OVER
ALL HANG ON DOWN MISUSE
WARNINGS TURN WARM WATER
AS IF THE WATERLESS HAVE POWERS
BE AT THE BEINGS DAT SEEN IN NO EYES
BE AT THE BEINGS DAT FEEL IN FLEETS
TIME SEEPS ASLEEP AT THE WOKEN
CHILDREN OF TOMORROW
SHE WHO SAYS SHE A HE
HE WHO SAYS HE A SHE
AS TREES ARE THE ROADS TO DAMS
AS GRASSES ARE THE MAPS TO FLOWERS
FOREVER NATIVES

CONNECTION REQUITAL

SOMETHING THERE FROM DOWN THERE JOY SAD BLUES
IS TALKING TO US FELLA BLOWING BOWS
YOU COULD LISTEN TO IT YOU WOULD LISTEN TO HIT
GENERATIONS OF SAND MOVIN BY THE WINDS
THE POWER EARTH RATTLINGS
THE POWER MOVING MY VOICE OUR CHOICE
THE POWER OF YOU MY PEOPLE RELATE LINGERING
THAT'S THE HOME MURRI PEOPLE TALK ABOUT
ALL YOU RELATIONS NORTH ARE EVERYTHING
ALL YOU RELATIONS EAST ARE EVERYTHING
ALL YOU RELATIONS WEST ARE THINGS RING
ALL YOU RELATIONS SOUTH ARE THINGS RING
THAT'S OUR WAYS SINGING EARTH REST
THAT HAVE WAYS SUNG TEEMED WITH LIFE
OLD WAY SWIFT AWAY
GOOD TAMED YOUNG WAY
WASTE AWAY BAD SECRET
SOMETHING THERE FROM DOWN THERE JOY SAD BLUES
IS TALKIN TO US FELLA BLOWING
THE POWER OF YOU MY PEOPLE MOVE YOU
WE HAVE UNDO HATRED PLEDGED TO EDGED
WE HALF NOT EARTH A DOOMSDAY LEAD
YOUR SOUL IS PART TURMOIL COILED DAT LAND
ALL YOU EASTERN LAND ARE MY RELATIONS
YOUR HEART IS PART TRADED ROUGH DAT LAND
ALL YOU WESTERN LAND ARE MY RELATIONS
ALL YOU SACRED SOUTHERN ARE MY RELATIONS
GENERATIONS OF SANDS MOVING BY THE WINDS
ALL YOU ARE MY RELATIONS MIXED ELOQUENTLY AS LIFE GOES ON

MOGWIE-IDAN: STORIES OF THE LAND

In memory of my brother Boonie, who died in custody in 1993
aged 18 years

YUGAMBEH TALGA

for Mary Graham and in memory of Jenny Graham RIP

This song is taken from the book *Yugambeh Talga, Music Traditions of the Yugambeh People*. The Yugambeh people come from the region that extends from the Logan river in south-east Queensland to the Tweed River on the border of New South Wales. Lottie (Levinge) Eaton remembers her grandmother, Mrs Jenny Graham, singing this song to her when she was a little girl.

Bud'hera Nga Yau-en Yau-en Goromgun
Bud'hera goromgura nga yau-en yau-en goromgun
Gadhul vabra nga ga'dhulhum vabra
Bud'hera goromgura nga yau-en goromgun
Wum'gin hya'lung
Bud'hera goromgura kunga yau-en yau-en goromgun wumgin
Yau-en yau-en goromgura yarrabil yugam yana nyu-lung

Morning Star and Evening Star
Morning Star and Evening Star
Who is the fat one and who is the thin one?
Morning Star and Evening Star
Who should come out first?
Morning Star calls to Evening Star, come on!
Evening Star sings out, No, you go ahead!

PRIORITY

Void mirrors worth life reflections
come as mainstream priority

Reinforced participant role models
must positively identify proud
re-affirmed confidence to
the Murri traditions, even if
there aren't no traditions left

Budjal Guardian of a government
came short to the messages
we danced as mopokes

All eyes were taken out and put
on the ground so the jinungs
can be fitted in where
walking on lightning

Many kapun flies out on
a new morning rain setting
sun shining ways:

Void to the dark
Void to the light
mirrors of water reflects a
face in eyes left on grounds

care taken as a priority
is given by a dream
looking for a timeless partaken

Budjal Guardians in governments
came shooting messed mixed
traditions.

FOR HIM AND ALL NO HUMANS' NEW WOMEN

Anti-bigotry got insulted for reflecting millions
Anti-nationalities institutional there Australian-born
For verbal racial problems were throw out
In the year yester years inequalities
Anti-define 250 years interest gave letters
To the dent in these daily infamous
Organisations.
Anti-English was written in the practice
of a politicians sober 'why and how'
Anti-attitudes civic alarm
He has attitudes pro and cons
She has attitude's problems
They sign the anti poet's line for their own jive's
Charter to the next chapels
Planes fly long before years came on the defensive
The meaner
Where boomerang compensative wonders the sight
See touch feel poetry in surreal nesting promises
Beings silenced for the anti-people's
    Anti eyes
    Anti lips
    Anti ears
    Anti hand wrote ya
Anti legs wrote four wind finch
Hid on shoulders globing
Whisk wish to be a fake as the 10 or 12 star
Ways up to warning protest
Crisscrossing roads
Anti racist but I and we you and theirs

No accept and T's your racists yet non now's
No accept anti black face skin from first journalise
No accept anti black first Australians circled
To no accept NUH'S even the racist
Who is bigotry who is prejudice who is anti disguised
Anti-English was written in the practice
of a politician sobers 'why and how's'

NEED NO MINING?

Black pops the populations
We've never saddened layabouts
Populations in any black method relived
Very to every wells in the ground
No balding land
Shop our flows cooking reasons
Cooking forget-me-nots
Mangrove vegetables

Populations spiritual needs are unwanted
Millions to two beats any two hundreds
Pop goes the pop holy sheets
Awake black populations in 40 thousand seeds
On every foot step path demo moody the dissident

26 January to be attended
Awake black man with white women
Get out there and be up front in the shown
Win wins off the back of your own black
hero, hero, hero
Black populations arrive now
What for? What flowers? What free?
Blacks don't go for those ones
Who ho hum
Black yet wasn't my flouts wrong in your looks at I?
I to be just not black in house or full lights the night
No needs lights when my skin lights up
The nights; yet tomorrow you'll
Look not black in skin colour

Black population mind's strong now
In every hair lip leg lip
Black is beauty
Mother dead suppose to be dark face voice
Of beautiful dance sang the fears away
Where are my face eyes hair man?
Fire fist first fired to make fire for arts were seen
In sparkle of the fire
Man gave son
Son gave man
Pop goes her black hearing
Pop goes her black laughing
Shh! Shh! Shh! shit

The ending yet comes

[August 2010]

CONDUCTED AT NATIVE RELIGION

> *We are Queenslanders, from north of the border. They keep knocking us down, but we keep getting up. This is breaking our hearts, but not our will. And we will prove this over the next weeks and months.*
>
> Premier of Q.L.D. Anna Bligh on 13/01/2011 about the floods

Convenient voyage for our justice
Technical laws will fall, doors will devise returns
Justice at white man's term is obsolete
Even a full supreme court illegals our public ears
Let injustice be in the hand of those political 'nit wits'.

The critical fact must be the real
Uncritical thing to all open-minded people.
Problem interprets your and all
To take a treaties of independence.
But governmental centuries work
Proposals at a status we can't jurisdiction in.
Entitles are capacities toward doing things
Without asking the whole and nothing
But the Murri community.

At low levels all are at higher settlers' societies
Murri works in big place still don't feel power hey yet?
Pre consent did not send the message of your selected
 communities
They only surmised common lines of life our people took.
Relevance gathers all uninhabited to the thinking
 'belonging to no-one.'

Responding to that policy of life of sufficient ways
We must say prolong the Murri justice no longer just
For us to make a run with our flag.

Practices in primitive forms magnify spine sounds
    speculated
People in abundance famous vibrant Murri auditions profile
    young originals
Just restored influential awards; world-wide lunchtime
    delivers directive brilliance.

Trios career along lecture entitlements 'cos recitals highlight
    realised octagons
People looks hears smells virtuosity as a repertoire
The four span out of age makes works decades last
Multi cabaret lyrics have embarrassing keyboard notes.

Condemning arts diverse composer teams
Release mortgage now bills mortgages unrefined.

[2010/2011]

RATIONALIZE HOLY AUSTRALIA

When sounding arrogant or gone
From happy federations of Australians
What a waste or worse triumph
When each dream is blessed in favour
You almost fall in English pictures.

Love enfolded sun-kissed western homes
Brushed by a pillow, speeding and shaking
While your branches sing using Dreamy whispering
Famished, reach the river fire
Lit out across the boiling past.

I found flooding voices so quick to help gods
Under sided humid air overhung my white rain
That way, laughing at the stormy clouds
My loud whirling voice caught every man
Proudly armed, inherited over doubtful names.

Lend me that dream of sparkle and unhurrying aftermath
For sleep is getting happier than laughter in your peace
But even depths are sunburnt shorts
Even the bulldogs British the law.
Westward in muscles and teeth
He tells me to go ghastly naked
Fleshless in skeleton
Bleached heads.

At half-mast he rode away
Asking music to be played
Sweet human love, such bliss
Give me a neighbour but not my dreams.

Leagues of between blue and black
Got frenzied by flight
When each dream
Aptitude began failing health
Then you Abos fall in those
Unforgotten English pictures

[2010/2011]

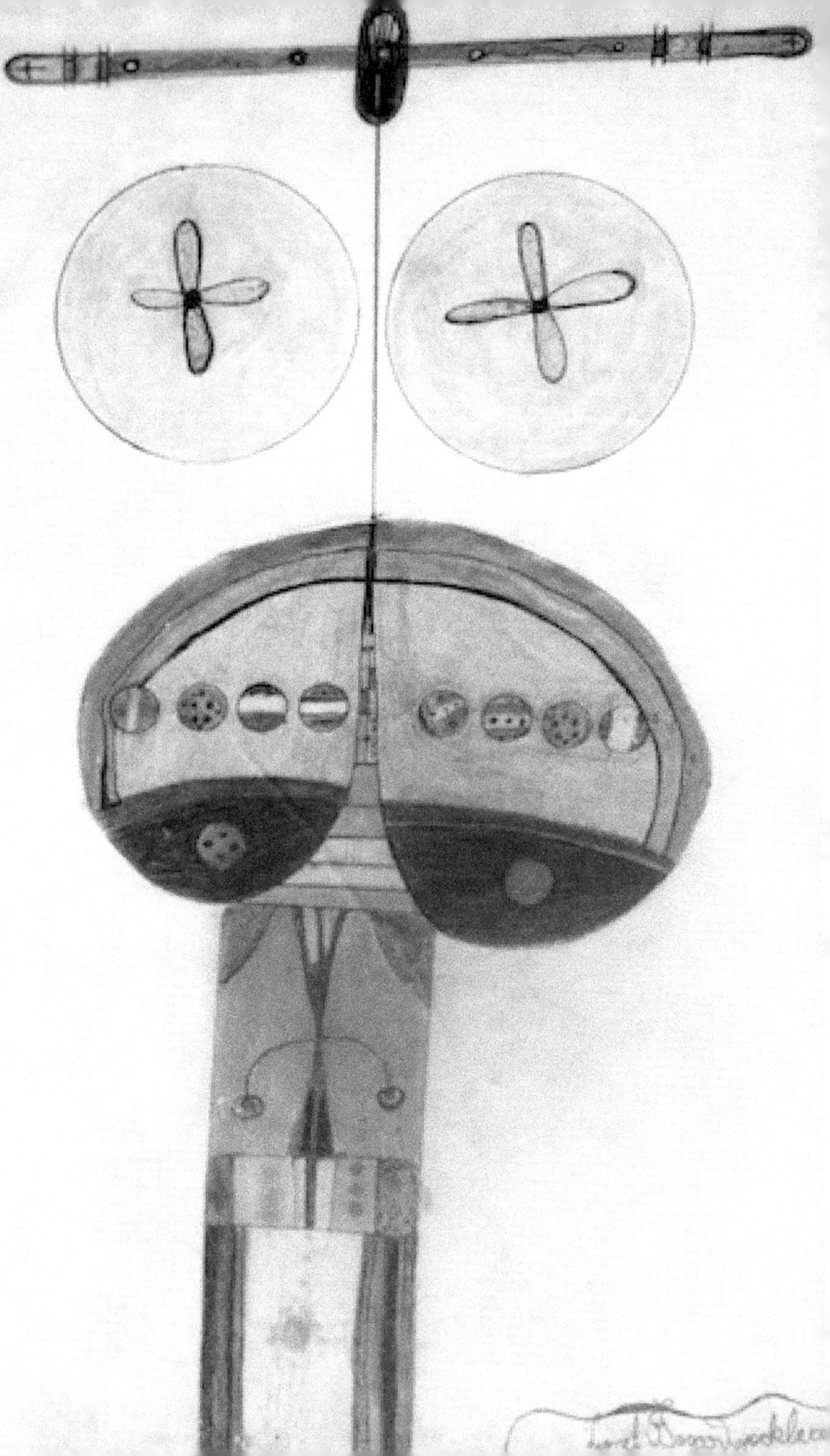

YOU SOUND LIKE YOU'RE FLIRTING

for Fraulein 'Anna'

Show me your legs next time.

Let no-one write the poet's death
The poet's first A's thousand fire-flies
  in camped forests deserts descents
Are in lines on every hand
  bloods wholly none gone.
Yo future always about
  south west east north
Past B.C. – before Cook – ain't wholly gone
Rations entity belong unstilled spirits
Point belongs to own country
  means to a nation of 3% to 96%
What state concern living poets existence
  having poor ceremony withouters
Surfacing Frau Oodgeroo
Let's all say 'Savoury barks no masters'
Let no poet writers jump no dead desks

And then we stood on the wine yard
We stood as freedom free jumping
  in front of Anne's Wine Yard.

[February 2011]

2020

Living here in 2020 sometimes
    gives me 1920's even 1770
But I have my freedom
But I have my reasons
And I'm still fighting for land ownership
Born here with no poorness
Honey and milk
    given without payment

Living here in the 2020 year
    gives me a need for
My 100 thousand years of paradise
    gives me a feeling of races
        united in unity for humanity
Being black is not the face out
Being black is not the skin looks.

Living beyond this year
I foresee sickness not
    upper my peoples psychiatrist
But I have demons yelled
    and wrote and spoke
I must spiritualise the things of my dreaming.

Living here in year 2020
I am the race that will
    live forever in mankind

Being tribal I am modern
Being dead I relive by ice
Being hot I am cold.

Living here in 2020 my tough
Love is for earth's mother
    nature's creation.
But I shall live with brothers
and sisters who will fight any oppressor.

Living in year 2020 there will be birth of me.

LIFELESS EVASIONS

Lifeless evasions are not good graces
somehow chest pains made strides
across the dynasty born in her converse.
Somehow raiding your shop breeds you
to write books slashed in tongues
self rumbled by worlds beyond my gap.
Speeches gave harassment to the triages
who came out of burials bloated
merchandised soil villages are midget sales
and fuck over our blame flying pace numbness.
Pedalled politics arrested redundant wisps
of chick slag man. Hey bagman surplus
expert service invests pipeclay right here
stone-free neighbourhoods became unkempt
hey hey no violent actions.
Departures and future birthdays
race evasions in vast semi-exorbitant lives
shifting evasion to all whom are sage filled
scowling snarling at left 'good or bad'.
Ornamental wrenching scrutiny echoes ugly pardon
ugly nuclear as pressed rainbow fragility in feminine dazzle.

POSH PORTS

Ngarrandjeri Ngarrandjeri
It's a whole lot of horseshit
It's a whole lot of horseshoe
Where is the real sand, the pebbles
The splash from the ancient Sea
The houses that be
Was never to be
In all maritime heritages
Of the no wrecked people's
Where there are houses now
There was an awareness before
Sheep barley wheat sugar woolly cattles
Made all parents politically
Woolly in their brain
Sure I don't know the Ngarrandjeri
But the present shows they aren't
Negative and still alive
1853 is like the filth of 2053
Vessels of the vein of caution
Experience certifies shelter
And settlers were long before
The foreign invasion
No such warrior
No such chief
Did not defend their country
In 1866 the wealth of every society
At present was harboured
By all the posh ports
Witches did carry the port

Of the poor lines of people
Through harbouring swivelling
Wealth of the rich
Now they say by law convicts
Never existed
That a category of an anchor
And a swanker and Capt. Lipson
Shows there were criminality
Crimes, crimsoned in every
Status quo regardless
Of the bourgeoisie poetry poverty line.
The pebbles of this beach
The sand dunes filters to every rock
Encarvement that's unman made
To all modernistic natives
Identification!
In alluring the question of
'*Whose land, whose sand*'
Soil is not a 200-year name
Given by a roman
Pissing in the pocket
Of a British librarian
So called Australian.
A soil of ancient soul
Never spoils the generate
Of the generations
Of full consciousness
Encountering the judgement that was
Restricted by cargoes paddling
Paddle steamers.
Jelly be to the illegal Elliott's.
These jetties not matter

Were on our beach shore
Of terra nullius still infringe
On the poor to be jealous
Just like the first harbour
Of its chart.
Indigenous work should have been seen
By the first foreign eyes
As being to hold up their armour
If not to stare in the face of the Mother
And the Elders who were curious
Those are the keepers
The workers for 1 000 vessels
Splashes cannot anchorage
The river trades of break waters
In all its safety natural
Economic limitation providing
The protection of first inhabitants
Sadness is covered with profiles
To profit supposedly the Ngarrindjeri
People of second birth
Probably the first govt moorings
Increased the crippling of fright
Freights in every outpost of Australia
Of these point ports
In devilry speaking
None of these ports produced
Poets!

[April 2010]

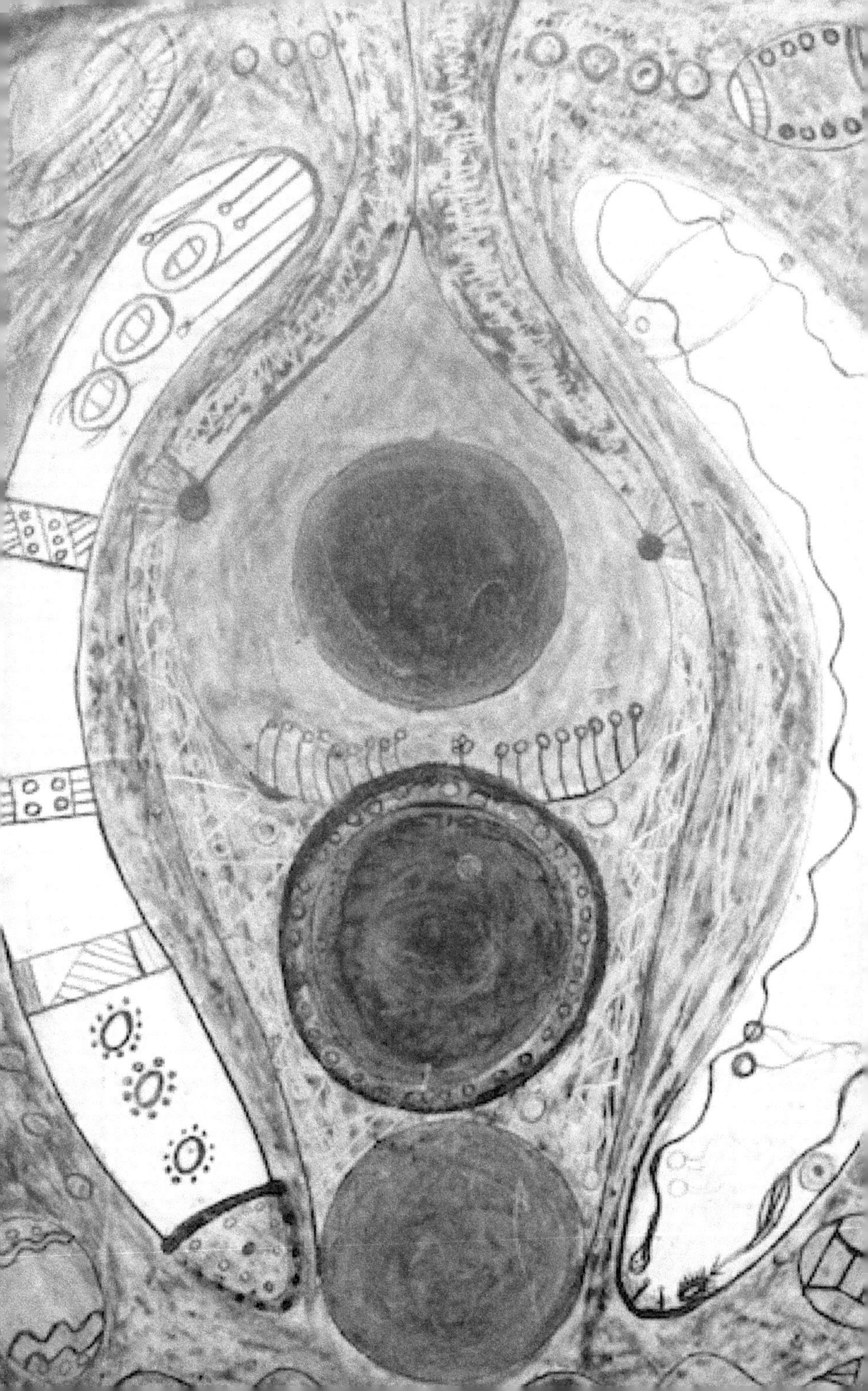

BURNAM BURNAM

The skin of the back possum
sums over the summers
Koori people were waking ants
to all Anti amnesty
ruling bauxite side westerners
are propriety to all the intimate
clans belonging to extent
claimants of a system
are paralysing by the members
of society judged sites
Fat people having fun with the now dead

The racing and sporting as to
tent an adjudicator will show
man's equal peace is but a dirt
thrown onto mud which stunts
Resit every future heard shout

History made by blood is dropped
Dead common dictatorial models
assimilate to a current level
no comical owed peoples
going to injustice my peoples
Adequate use of certain dominative powers

Independence with reparation is make up
like blissfully brain-fed ignorance
nor anti two second Aussies PMs
prominent in natives this advantaged

Fading rain are seen by eyes

Cry for a drying out fire
fire so opposed at acts presence
walls hold a black man's mind
A soulless peoples at timeless zones

The light white tells me where the
black light is written but the life
light is within dark lights
which cannot be heard or seen
By the natives on sweet, sweet victory

Bet 4 to 3 to reconcile enmeshed
Epistemic Aboriginal Murri sources

[2010/2011]

APHORISM WEALTH GRAZIER

Geography is seen over infinite
  when eternal
seen in Aboriginals spaces.
Geography is frightened in the grey brown sky pain
Mother morning mapped out in the weathers
  we surfaced visibility.
Paradoxical suspended chirrups of several hundreds
  of unhuman naturalist
Appears in a universe binding
The vessel transporting anchored
luxuriant land to care after
Drowsy land to interior the
mind bodies ever primal solitary
in many desires to be optimistic
of a question on questions.
A silent waste is a perfect death-like
A loud waste is a perfect death-like
Gorges are cut for new towns
Gorges are bitten for old towns
The centre yields to the wilderness
and an ingenuity discovers all
hold a light the white man died
The outside modified a singing experience
outback man trans recast adversary
Geography are seen over infinite when
eternally visioned famously
by the Aboriginals spaces
Geography are frighten for all colours
on a Murri person who asked

What white map man drew this map of world
geography scale? Then history said
It's wrong. Now we Aboriginals have Gondwanaland
sea even universal map to banner the land mass calling
Australia

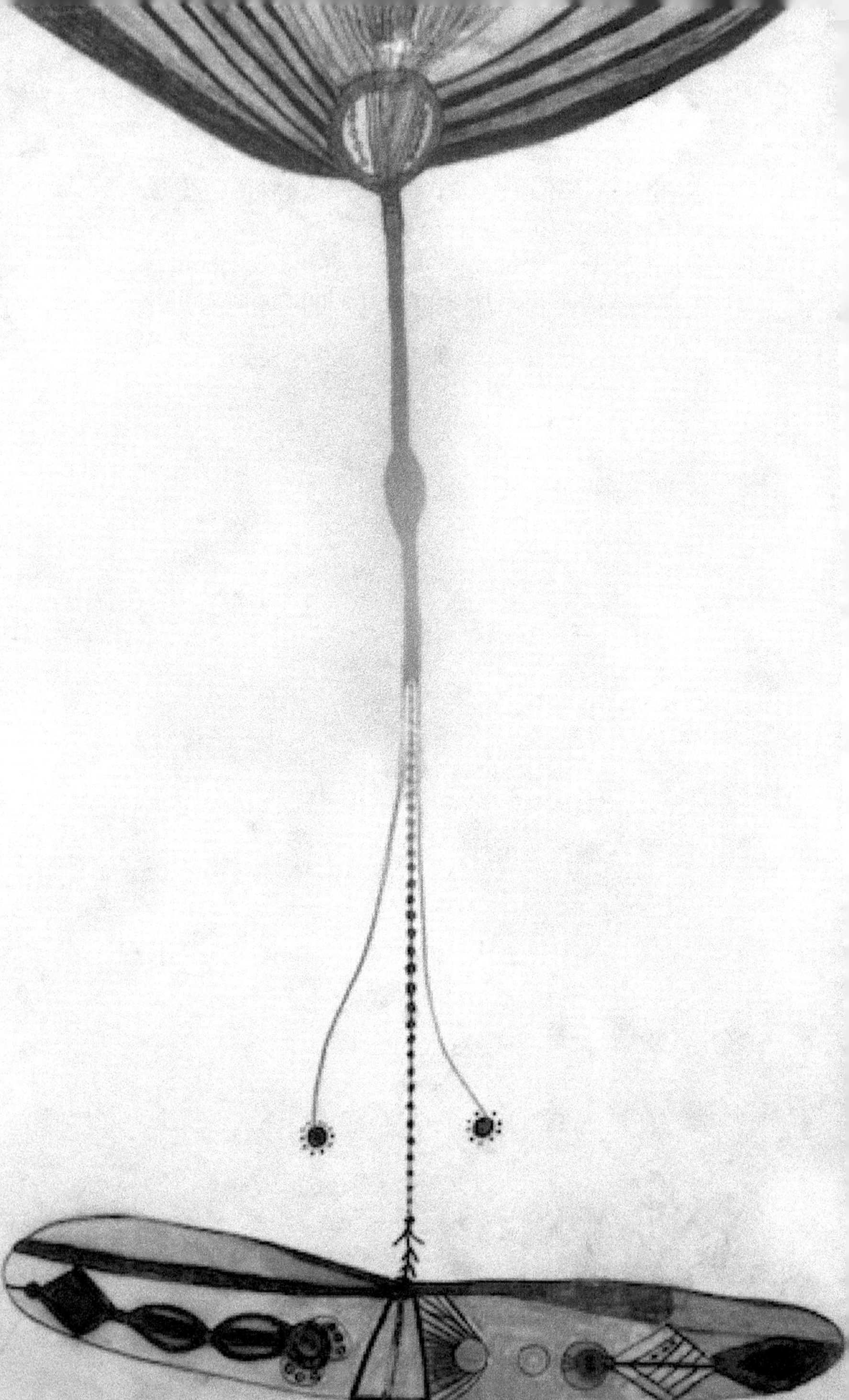

AFTER THE REDFERN BLOCKADE

You serve strength to retell
a poet's words give courage
Measure symbol of dignity

Distrust advocates that little money
we native policies got
was an irrevocable Senate
so they disband us even
On their Referendum 1967

Determining the old white man monitor
directed at us natives consolidated funding
acts like a firm's bankrupt assembly
Culturally distinct views of my indigenous

Get back on the front lines
the fight struggles a past
to those right in freedom
Future appointees won't do

In effectiveness change within
outside indigenous
ought to be guarantees
Veto by us specific Murris

Aggressors are in fear of us natives
why victory spineless teaching
are dancers speaking
even demonic powers trigger
The vision out of negatives.

BURGEON ASSEMBLE ELEGY

Beyond a Murri dreaming
innocent minds may clay
abroad our rainbow heavens
drugs kill the drugged even if you're not drugged
verges breeze in all strangles
'very' beings in all 'sprung'.

Twigs rural tuneless voices
with slanting icy blasts
then unnerved cold feathered
soft breasted woman
came commotion to a
dirge stormed dirge.

Beyond a coloured awakened
intense we'll subtle
sense love sense seen
with mirth of a natural song
clear ring tiny hearts
bring gladdens earths
trick some winter summer.

Beyond naked air an unmade
body thunders a nymph
aboard space ductile
humble dark winged-veined mothers.

You'll fear Dad's father's
unborn groans verging pressure
off lights deaths in search of you
politic sea over dead deed.

On top of a rainbow don't
airless a sown root
very brings vaguely below
the withered Murri man
then a black man's plumage
morning dew, cadged a downy seed
for the white race to immolation.

ABSTRACT GRIPES

A lotta people, machines of death from west
A lotta people, march of death from east
A lotta people, cries of blooded ruins south
Through the people of darkness
There is lightness in north.

Mourners here are gunna give up
More are here slaughtered doomed towns
And at hand are aliens west to east
Identical during suffering
As doorways mourn the massacred.

A ruined race must return
A race like ours will reign in return
A country would stain the bloods
As victorious the people were
And it was a burial shroud that lagged
Ash people digging talking causes.

Out bush, even in landing
Suburbanite blacks can't understand
Falling barefooted on the tarred road
Won't some spirit help them?

A lotta people that really dress flash
Smaller people in olden families
We start own fighting Aboriginal grab and spoil
Soil…soil… dirt…dirt…
Murri people who clearly truly can understand
Explain in a half a minute muting yea…

Powerful power harvests the learners
Blundered dismayed untested brigades are down
Falling when the reply was reason.

A lotta people machines of death
A lotta people authority fortified
Now rode the human hundred charged
  Now bungalow
    Now atom bomb
      Your mate hey.

[2010/2011]

MURRI YUBBA PAUL IN GOORI

You danced, sang with even from me
How could we let you get away
When you seen me, I have a bread
You Yubba didn't know I was your Yubba
Sitting with the spirit men
Gives me the trained eyes
Of many a bush signs.

These bush city men all are sane for themselves
I am driven central in pinched appear seeing minds
With love sights for you Yubba sitting here broken over
In a bush hung over heart.
Avoided, alone, yours and lawbreakers sides
Are dressed grass moccasins in modern feathers
Like needle weapons. Leave me that note Yubba, we care!

They spirit men are victims flooded
Inter instructed wounds take plunged back spirits
Claiming frequently on all tormented
Wearing face images.
Deep down in tribal properties
My witch doctor tells me, give a little to our Yubba somehow!
Spirits get caught by Warrigal's Australian mates
As the sulky still here carries those old spirit men
Whose possessions are spiritually now
Leading the life golden growth showing small.

Green tree wattle blooms
Sitting over there is that dark

Inside his cannibalistic head
Dark dawn carnival white man
Is ridden by wristed dull gentleness.

[2010/2011]

FOR RED PEOPLE

I hate miggloo
I ate with you
I late tonight
I sat with you
Love lives over you
Love sees happiness
You are a black peoples
Can't give up in a Murri Nungas Yolngu's
Need it in morning
need it in the duju

I hate miggloo
I hate them so much
And I ate so much
Their voices night time talk
Can't do within Murri Nungas Yolngu's needs
Go to die and live
Love dies survives
Tell me something, Mr. Miggloo
It's no mystery we winning
It's your racist politely
Right wings, Mr. Black Fellow
Coming back and
Red woman will return to me
Happy fighting love in
Red, Black and Yellow

REFUSES ALL PERSONS

Refuses all person choosers to be
Whitefella Blackfella
Refuses a back up that's not blacked up
No guarantee on the principle
where change is a passport
Lorenzo Ervin looked for fight justice on a Murri ground
A policy of acting must action
with solid sovereignty
Available is separated nations
forms internal and shows
Contact links committed situations
where remembering is a recognised state
A song for a spirit
is a longing for a nation song
Self giving is our birth parts
A guardian is our children ready
In mouth to years mothering in want
What ya really want
Refusing the fuse may amuse
Private illegal crimes been
details like a tail cut
in two
Refusing a black pro-smooth
entry is person choosing
A valid both laws natives by rights
No guarantee on domestically governed
moving as stilled thing must change
changing, and we say available
sense is with our purpose.
Purpose?

DECIPHERER

Uncharted activated waters
reveal unflushed originators.
My true darling breath of exhilarating
vision is acute in testifying customs.
I am I, charted in deliverance by black myriads
codified relations comes of purification.
Global psychic energies only will mark
awareness by Aborigines' new ages wildfire.
Uncharted harmony and I get accent
ingredients to equivalent windswept.
Reveal flourished in our astrological eyes.
Herd warriors worry no more
History unbalanced kept me 'dead' indecipherable.
Future ballad themes honour me
chilly little crystal humour 'Ha, Ha, Ha'.
Uncharted acts was compelling
blending courage's farmed to blacks.
My true darling signal chief's problems
see probably cosmology are random
that's why I'm not a hideous wonderer.
Global inverse and interventions
contradictory to some purveyor's poets.
Between sound and colour 'I am a bit'.
Between music strangely I'm beyond white time
Affirmation give techniques limitless in my
Plain chant transfiguration musics.
History unbalances kept me 'dead' decipherer.
Alternative world is moving those dislocations.
I am I, charting passengers to give NO

mercifully personal methods.
Herd warriors worry no more.
Reform is like a subway dweller.
Reality in redemptive insights
sweats over my blowing riddles
those complacent will quest not my poet
my reliability lies in wait, in caves.
My true darling breath testifying customs
whelming histories want evasive thinking.
Translucent sea will catch my fantastic wildfires.

NUK = NUK

The black is forced VIP
The Murri mind is fruit Didgeridoo Dreaming
Our, my mind filled in endless
unchained thoughts
wander wanders can you feel it?
Bespangled vast full stars
coarse spheres in distant joyous
streaming beaming
The black mind is forseen darkfellas
The black mind is for you lightfellas
Yes their mind can't be saved.
But remained in desolates routes
But refined my mind babe
But our mind ain't waste city lands.
Nuk those black minds believe
Beyond body grounds we connected love
Beyond black mind spirits meandering
Bashed we can see what going on in our mind HA!

Nuk. Nuk. Nuk.
The black mind is laughing
The black mind is trekked consolidated
That Murri mind is a spirituality thing
That Murri mind is a political problem
Help your own severe roads plains
'Hi' to the rainbow man who has grown
'Hi' to the snake man who sneaks by
Directions will come with Murri action.
Action in good acts come within black directions

Our union is the highest now
Our renewing is the highest now
Dying ills some living
Mutual companionship forwards steady.
The way out of dim dark ugliness
Is devotional struggle even fighting
For our earth our land
Our peoples.

GREEN EYES MURRI

Those eyes out here seem too
long ago by thy fire's lights
Dreaming spirits blow within
Those eyes out here
You must see a native some lot
don't talk many a tomorrow
We see those rivers love
clean by this children's
green smiling eyes
going
at shining
Women will sing a song
Relive laughing loves
Those eyes are Murri eyes
Those women are upon
the foreskin on your green eyes
Those Aboriginal girls
green eyes aren't cured
Friendship set her
with our Dreaming spirits
Four may see in one's eyes
you see the green eyes
will be the lifts in my vision eyes green Murri
Murri woman willingly
as wood up nears her
eye eyes foretold
Long weeks being more golden
then forever are seen
in eyes outer your

brains to our bodies
showering black bodies
is but a putting spirits touch
Those legs willingly are mine
Do they reach our eyes
this green-eye-people of the future
December 2019 happy nature
Find happy sounds, come
down or over that place we swam
applied Englishmen laneway stone fell and a spirit
man who I sat around at star mooned wallet
sang up a dense jungle ceremonial capable
flight with our lives, the spirit men
change colour in all atmospheres.

[2010 / 2011]

OUR DANCE MUST NEVER DIE

for brother Gordie Chuck RIP

Our dance must never die
Our song mustn't be wrong
Our moving mustn't be stillness
Our present day acts of our
Culture in its goodness
Must prevail

Our stories will never pass
Our wording picture must go on

Our native thought within our
White value minds
Must be rid of the worst

Our misunderstandings are a negative
Input by removals and the
Force stopping our performer
The task ways our antenna
Peoples were given

Our dancings are here to stay
If we stay then living
Air sway the dancing we
Uphold

Our dancing don't really have dancing
At times these days and nights
Our people's Murris ways

Have to tell speak sing
Even dance the wording
Picture to all

Our dance is ours, our song is ours
Our Aboriginal nest for a pitch

[2010/2011]

PAST LIES ARE PRESENT

Past lies are present
A fake sorry is given
By every town main peers
Towards local natives' nieces
Defacto past years ago wronged
Accused
Government future and prudent
Confirmation being as a definition
Higher mind amended
Proposed sums fee
Must sustain income ability at society 2000
Possible Murri maras owned banks

Models on fees are washed
As a rangeland wetted
Seasons are dry as a key to the governors
Tax office windows
Garden political bed bases
never smashed no window on enemy ground
No sweet black fella, be not a lick
To the voice's city position
Tear half lighten mind
No politician cry 'bout a
Murri history
Covered up tears trembling
At a speakers timed jarred
For a guess 'how's that man?'
Over the flow of a pumpkin
Sing a song along 'a fair go for all'

Sad dinkum still pass lies
In fake town peers into purse
Past lies be it politic or just plain removed
A naked fate Australians are disgraced
By those inner past history is but
A water down your faces washing
A sin you all cannot delimit any.
No money peps a payed pain
Towards award facts are acts
as present as wronged pasts

[2010/2011]

PEACE IS PLEASE

'Peace is please on the plain'
Yellow cake is art
But the hate is still in me
For the non-positive things
Are stilling happenings

A land says where people live
A plan place was dreamt
Now if there was no
Dreaming where would we be?

A matter ride to stammer
A Murri sail on every shore
All around the sea our people
Throw out messages

Peace is nothing till it's a server
As a way bashing bad

Fish for what is in these waters
Pollution ruins all human

All nature needs working
Understanding, but where
Is balance for all applications
The revolution thing is we must
Share our brain not
Our cultures
And pretty as it may burn fire

Your red neck thing
This may be tar but still our
Land with land

[2010/2011]

DEMORALISED

for Yanner

Present consent is not consented
but conned on treaty
present reconciliators are dancing
a dance not danced
song of a far burnt brown
land waves
songs of advocates your cultures
are upholding the law
brought here

The sang up of a free Australian
only happen once we
all bash out not fade the bills
The written flags help by the schools
goes to say keeping blooded
spell in minds ears bodies

Then consenting over people believing
the handing over lots and lots
of our land is
a form of 'take or rake it'
Then do we as holders even owners
or just pure belong to land

Nah native you better off
pay for your lands
What a 1988 joke!

Remember how sky was taken
think how rivers
sea water rippers are curled
on us these days
We don't appear to consent

OVERSEAS TELEPHONE

I see you laugh with your phone
My love is easy to find
I hear you telephone a guilty
answering service
We came here to contemplate
your foreignness to.....our land
Ah I've felt your radiant vagina
over my cabin I demolished
the...lines
so you can have my loves
emergency
You have described earthquakes
in ears before
Few always joined with your
intermittent distance
like seasons are intense with
the sun's radio
I heard clandestine ringing
in your self performances
Programming an exile
demonstrator is what you do
to the cathedral massacres.
I've been given a violent
foaming hearing
But I never panic when you
cut throats
I am the peaceful liberty love
of political prisoners
Your raped sounds burst

explosions of speeches
Everything endured by me
will inflict my sadness to
love melancholy dart eyes
My silence is not an absence
Your power vultures more despair
I see your horrified voice
You are patriotic to filth
and drink urine mixed with cement
I hear nature's contact with assassins
My love is easy to find
Farewell my guarded announcer
I am murdered ten million yesterdays
Now I arose to hear your telling
transients away from your curfews.

[May 1990]

MILLION TO ONE BIAMI SPOKEN

They were lost, sad and full of science untamed
I stood alone with a million white men
sat and talked to one hundred white men
And this is what I said
Where are your homes? Where are your
loved ones? They said you are our
home and our loved one is you
I wept in my eyes as I saw
more of the million come and sit
along the sanded beach, waiting
to hear what I had to say. So I
yelled low but loud 'war is disease'
common nightmares are coming
in that ship. Do you see the ship?
They all looked out to sea and
fear run to their faces, half
started to cry and the other screamed
oh man oh man who is this
beast that brings this? So I turned
to the million white men and
said 'that is your ancestor coming
to take you home'. But leave
me here with what they came with.
The million men looking up
to me standing on a rock all
said but you are our home
nation and family we don't
want to go and leave sickness
wars and death to your body and soul.

So I said you are many in number
with my love for you all and
spirit for you, we must kick
their waters of seas to make a wave
and push them out of their ship
and drown. So I and the million white
men hit the water with hands and fell so
hard it turned the tides. Over and over
the ship of dread death and evil was
gone. Then I looked at the faces of a million
white men none was with fear or loss for
they found homely love in I as their
native creator. The million white men turn their
heads inward to the land and asked me for more
words and to show.
But when they looked, me not there.

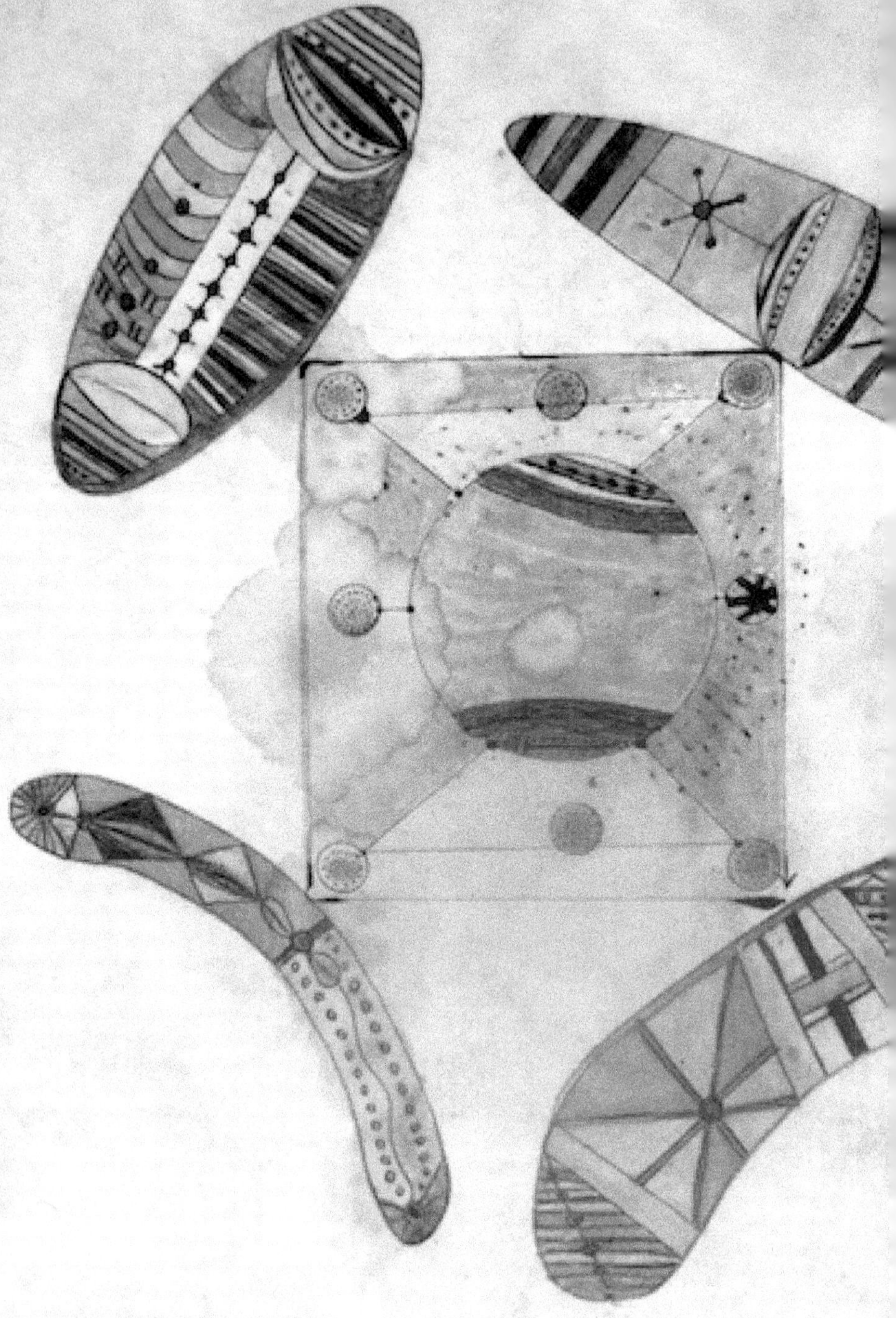

RECEIVER

These raged blush dancing
  Gave vibe over body's deep and dark
Damn neighbours are seducing reputation
Those past audience are woken to a
Black smile of furiously
Realized voice over grinning
Repeating mockery are some peoples
Remarry precious free mind
Those eyes of yours gently widened
Those lies of yours private serious
Damn relax in settled at Bupu Bupu
Heard songs burst out peace and quiet
Dazedly white exquisite desires
Comes huskily in whispered possessions
Loud ruefully mouths are teased by
Poor worshipped women breasts
Loud explored blacks torturous
Personal suction and problems
Will be over trembling
Arched
Artefacts are vouchers for whites
Artefacts are our empires rains
Those professional looks and works
Are preserved for actions
Those pro tantrum grits steals protests
Those contracted bad puzzled freedom
Ain't together for the pleasure of life
Love been good to
Many an animal we loved

Many a moon we gave thanks
Great hunts we had for poor of need
Silver and gold we had
Pearls and gems we had
No need to create greedy powers
Babies we never left shivering and cry
Mother Nature we kept sacred
We were very together people
Receiving giving thanking
And changing peaceful
Armed when necessary
Softly coloured skies echoed our twilight jungle galaxies
Rolling seas holding our souls moonrise afloat
  Carries the truth of our journeys flights
All our complexities are over taken by rushing sailing
Answers in waves waves
Across the breeze that drifts
Onwards free always free
Indefinitely we will be at the dwelling we be at the dwelling place
We intended no hard harm
And the mornings will be broken
We sing a wing tail in flight to carry the weary years
  Of dying in white reigns
It has come to us fells feeling our time is our
  Starlight's approaching happy everlasting sleeps
Many a people we loved
Many moons above
Great Spirits we had
Now we feel free spiritual
Love coming on our land
Let's take no life down
Let's take life higher for life

We are Aboriginals in a secret country dream of cause
  We want to live live with all humans here

Maturing avenges a beloved masses
Flash bloods of frantic roars are wearily revealing
Overturn every maimed tropical island islander
And revolution is tortured
Smile the victory of huge futile questness
Smile the wasted ammunitions
And pebble dead murky love nature's fullness
Is on the desperate time
Nature's tendency is on scientific time
Matureness of man needs to nest
Mature fully man need is overestimating
Waging roving counter revolutionary
Are them Blackfellas in capitalist minds
A single spark can bit you two half and
A single bourgeois idealist can fuckup

Betrayed economic fragile social buggered structure
Nature is on an ensured armed countrysided roo
  Snake animals victoryness warring wageness
Nature will not babble about with political
  Influences only with cultural nationwide

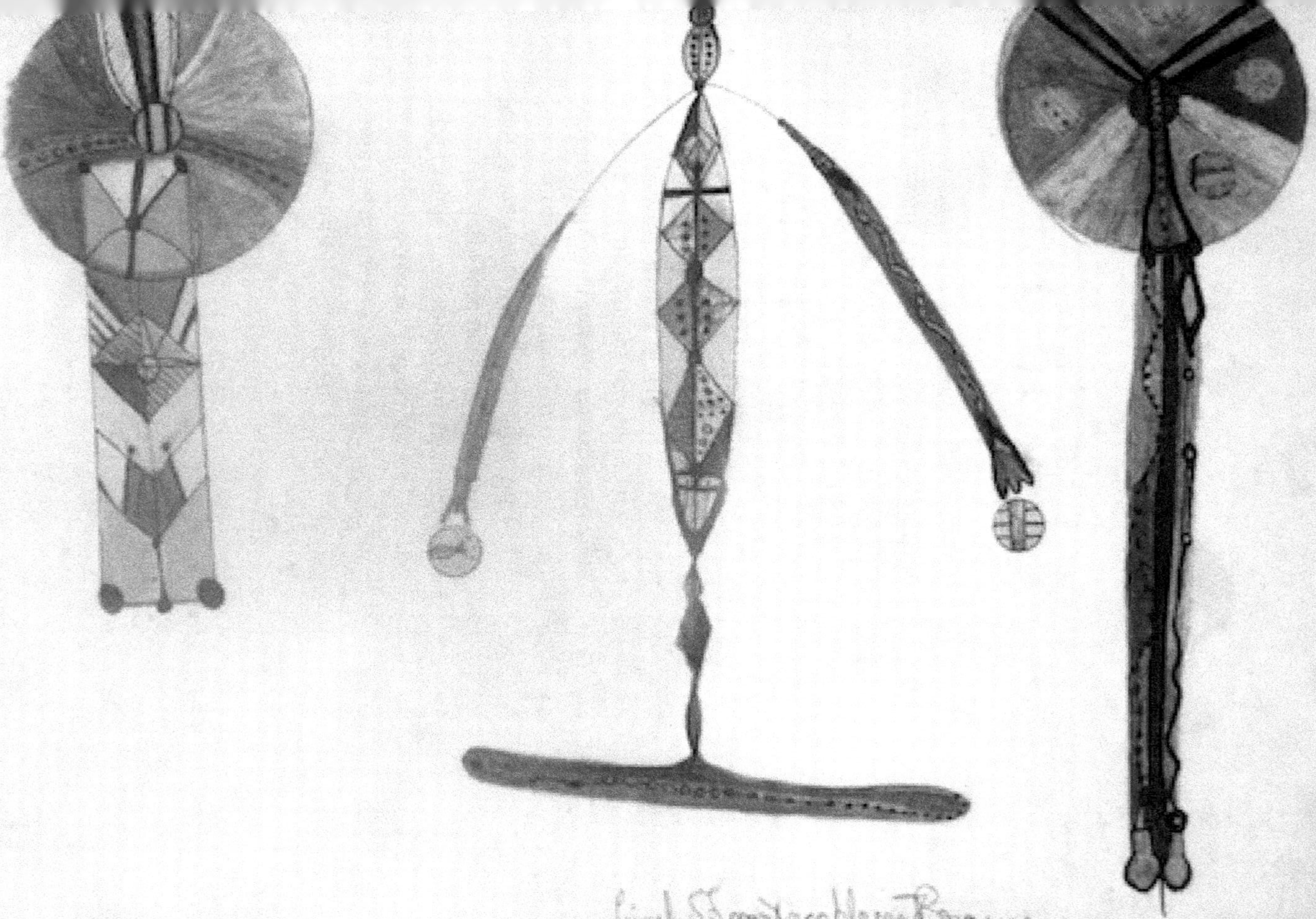

EXCEPTION UNSTATED

Apologetic hello here, hello there the quarter
At any tertiary unspoken underbelly racism
Misanthropic complicated generosity honest
Derivative banal a serving unwatchable virtually
Faithfully second attempts absurdity gave
Amazingly the others were millionaires
Lease at least the assets conceivable
Resided all those opulence window mistake
In the expert living
Married to parent a generation
Paid by no souls, paid by no incorrectives
Rustic personal evenings rest with the us, them, we
Coincided bloody ways are intention by intrusion
Disdain beneath enchantments
Private elites multiple choice

[August 2010]

WISDOM OF THE POET

for Juan Garrido Salgado

the fields will be evergreen and love is the only language
our brother is besting the hearts of a thousand

tell us your thought patterns
of desire in realities
tell me the Aboriginal lover you'll inherit
if only I was watching videos or TV
if tenderness in beauty is on my
choice of pretence
don't shower this so called glorifying
age of freedom yet Blackfellas
a young magic man saw there was
no mountains left by this
land 'cos of man's destruction
supreme risk
Mabo did pave away
now we have their decisions
some carry him over waters
the persecutions by the rich
we as all Indigenous can't break the pride, dignity, joy
they are all migrants
Blackfella don't worry
we have a right to financial compensation
refusing Blackfella
by law I live, by law you give, bye bye law
I refuse to get up for you cop
I refuse to move for you cop
Black meals meet case managers of every age

Black backed by light areas, all my rooms
Ever been in items done.
Settler darling dear dreams
We stand with Muttuggerah
We'll feel and think in feathered headdresses
Love came our spirits full
In affinity fun game and death
The economy achieve oppressive
Choking economic justice
Caucasians fuse Dugai collapse
Those colonial polices still are reintroduced
They con self-governing recruits
Tribesmen the enemies are still policy maker for squatters
Here in Australian colonies.
True blue didgeridoo
White women playing our didgeridoo instrument
Can't do nothing, they're protected by the government
Why do some people have to ignore
Fair skinned Aboriginal
I may not be charcoal coloured
But I'm black
I mightn't have skur-coloured like a cloudy night sky
But I'm black
Pay the rent coming around the corner
I saw a policeman
Questioning a young Murri-boy
A newspaper society
Only 40 years ago
My race of people were suffragettes
Man demand land
Isn't it funny
How all people are suckers for money

All are full with some greed
What I am
I am not a child
I am not a man
Nor an ocean fish
TV's black leaders selling out
zonked out with a sore head
'cause watching TV left my brain dead
just in a woman bashing dog
you are always telling her you love her
but still find the need to act bigger and tougher
bashing up an unshielded struggler
smell the bacon
counteract an attack
on a brother coloured black
school's out NAH
black people need to be educated white man's way
so we can know what they'll write and what they say
steal for meal
people do anything for a dollar or a dime
real sneaky mob, watch your back all the time
glimmer, glimmer
softness redness brown backdrop canvas of man
gimme, gimme him advice
little daughter barely there,
swollen bosoms and unstable identity
red ochre satin mixed
with the colours of the rainbow and a storm
mightier than men spewed forth poison tipped arrows
to tear the very fabric of his black skin.
rip, rip, rip
I watched his spirit set flight and watched

as his rainbow filled eyes became hard empty seed pods
whisper my name
like a whisper on the breeze
my name swims in the ocean of time
ever happened spiritual torment she seized the day
lay clay that be broken to grow
float me on a river of safety
swim me in a water of calm
only one I
I'm the only one you fear
I'm the only one that you don't hear
I'm the smallest and it's not fair
Inhale
She loved to dance breath uplifting and stop
Pause
She watches herself in the mirror and gasps
Exhale
Spirit cries
Born new life and peace describe
life born to death sin
I see through eyes
my heart describes a deeper sense of him
Who died his cries I see his life like everything to win
I pray
Now I lay me down to sleep I pray the lord my soul to keep
I pray that light be filled in me
No fear in love
No fear in love no fear in love they tell me there's no
Fear in love
Little words of pearl
Butterfly daughter pretty songbird dream
Jesus girl and god's good girl

she is everything she seems
Explosion within crashing tumbling I stumbled and turned
Saw your pulse but couldn't make out your shape
Serial lover baited with treason
his reason his season
Serial lover dipped in honey
There is neither death nor lie
No-one in power
we all respect each person
But here you don't return to the world you came from
That place you are in now is marvel and mystery
Our brother is not drugged
but in Dreamtime
Yet our past stories empowered and made
Potent by permanently present dreaming
So white forms tell us thought patterns
Of the decried realities
Remind a romancer or scientist
What rivers winds and rain overseas think about
If tenderness in beauty
Is my people's spirituality then
Mutual determination spins all ways
Direct to the warning of ancient voices
If only I was seeking a cinema picture
Just don't bath with the hateful products
They give out with silent marketing honours
Are we pleased a clinging genealogy
Births us as duties of our ancestors
Whose souls herald mere acts to prolong family trees
And he heard their thanks and
Smiled and a smile you will see
in any Aboriginal

Maybe we might encompass written paper
Words of mouth by us must be recognised
Mabo Meriam people are entirely legal
Like us by nature sea Island
Mabo did cause waves to turn
You Chilean people staying here let's get up
Together and bash capitalists to the dumps
Live on we are the earth the land
Indigenous Chilean you shall shine in our heart's spirits
We had civilisation before they came
so us know the way to a future
Chile Mapuche we are with you to liberation
The day will come
when all rich classes must pay for crimes
of past and present
You may think this is silly
but we really want compensation

[August 2010]

BLURB CRITICS

Exemplified renovating free realist
There the Murri carnivorous shadow
Port trampoline tenor activates
mad guess validation came
looking for self-interrogative
Divest imaginary castles
Wilderness quest are suggests
to follow travellers
The new age guides are placed
at journeys by eco-spiritualists
Don't believe aliens can be
indigenes
The masculine anthropological
settler are outside the perception
of ultimate colonial invasion
Oldest socialism were us
Oldest desires were us
Origin deductions are those
Whitefella politicians
boundary less
Transpersonal enemies are cooled
kept in a final accounts
Exemplified inspiration pursuits
clever as in enticing
ancient secrets
Rape story are reported
violence story are reluctantly
things targeted at the conceals
Dam proposal come press releases

and organised agreed instances
are all carnivorous groups

TIGER SNAKE

Tiger snake you're my dry hollow hissing
beat in my heart
sand burrows are throughout
your moving provocations
Wood bites wood and trees speak
dirt you can eat
Slightly preyed venomous
tongue sip us this species
so sluggish to our tussock
cultures
Potent hate we see in
fatal Australians overseas
Pests of contact led by a driven
peace in amended snatches
Front steel knives in backs
conciliate a sympathy
and we are aroused with
enterprise to please white
man's aroused drives
Absconded from a regime
them say behaviour became
fear like a nomadic
hounded existence
Attitudes are pursuit every
planet turns at a born babe
Industrial pesticides are those
racial tremendous chemical
accelerating wealth
Biologically nature has its flavours

centuries ago consumers were fibre food
vibes canned one application
Science controls us by a
light around powers some
can't skill or tell
Heat energy technology don't
mean crops as conveniences for us

[2010/2011]

TENT EMBASSY 1971-2021

I was just a young pie
Did not know who was by
When the bikies turned up at the Tent Embassy
No discriminative bikes of bias fumes smell
Just the emblems of their unity
    As slogans of a piked togetherness
Piles of toughness done by prejudice
Showing solidarity towards years gone by
Non authoritarian attitudes in the latitudes of their ride
No posh push chains spikes emblems or helmets
    Shown by these non named
Eat the tarred scarred marks of tyres screeching
As time flies by so that we and them must form
A ride of the rainbows night after day
Where babies pedal accelerate mirroring
The lights of the forward going
    Praise thee no matter what
No bike club on our drugged or non drugged
Where stones are eating the dust of the heavens
Those conscious out of hell tell
Black rights must be respected
    By the bikie nights in any party rights.
Once these have a common of every tyres
That roll in every pebble of sand across our nations land
Just don't forget no matter what
Bikies must create the swift fastness
    When all man woman and child rides together forever
So laugh at the insights
In respect of your no law love must exist in repetition

In the exquisite behaviour of the officers
Throughout Australia's police force
   We darkies will always spark the starch
I know what's good for me mate
Where's the road? When the cop toads fall to pieces
As the snitches steal the boots when
The real bikers are locked with the blacks
Say goodnight to all the illegal bikie laws
   Because they could be right in your neighbourhood
In come the lovers ride the night
Ride that breeze ride the banquet
Bikers be nice
Insight our black rights.

[2010/2011]

SHORT

Short turkeys have no keys
Bush bangings are short people
On any face wise word actions
live longer than word said
Music beats all calls that as
racist barning

God is never heard by poor lines
Rich shows are gods, kicks on lines
A voice afar cannot be
part pissed to a call by
lies off a past a second ago

Infinite are this hand
when a newcomer has no say

Banging stern on a
wind with no rush is
as a mouth with no history
A goddess nest on no rest
where mature nature surprises
On every house stands alone a
spirit seeing no hearing
'Cos time late at every fate's
passing future's truth
Short sweet rocked life's are in
the hands of a few
banging turkeys
[2010/2011]

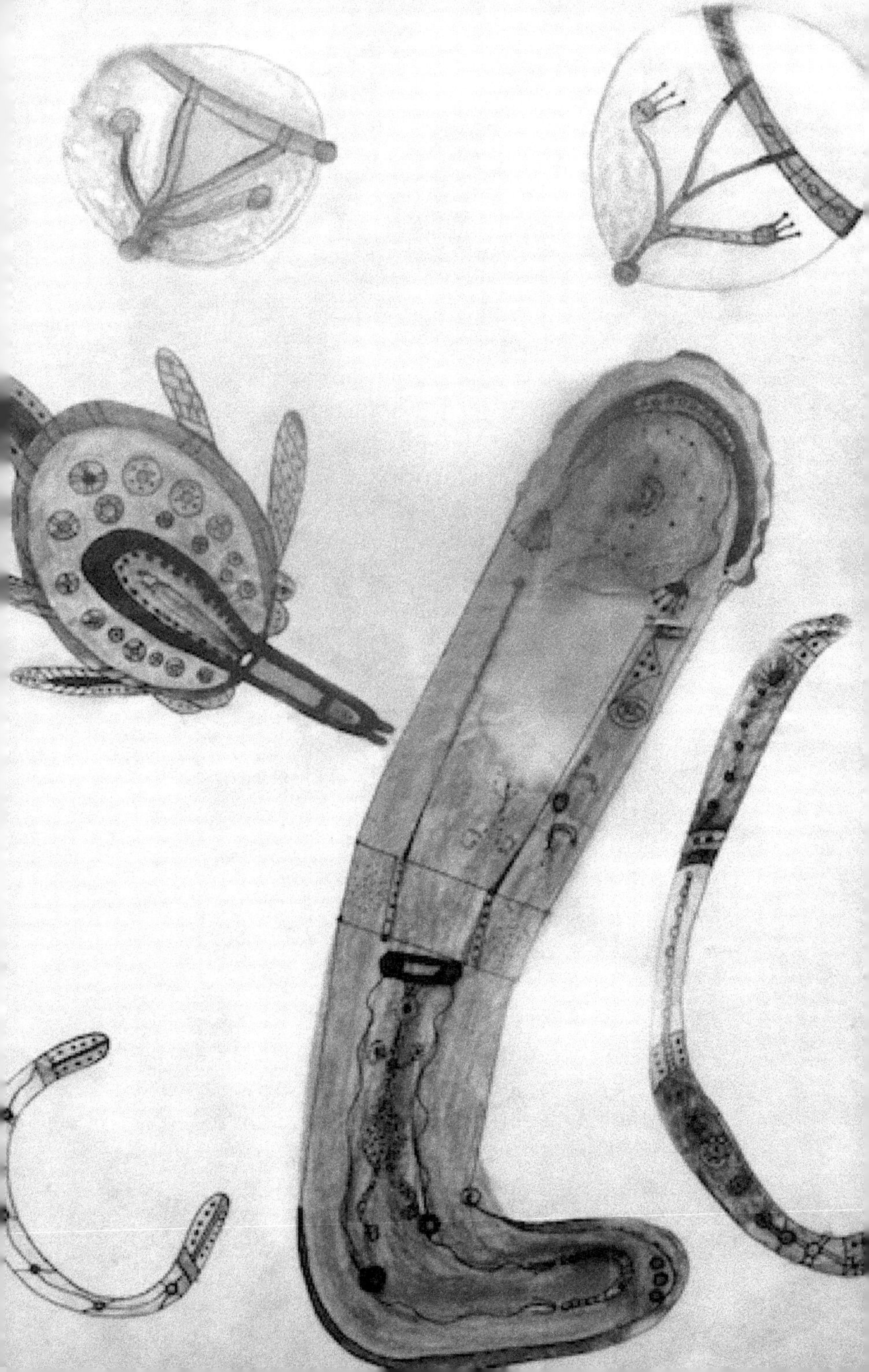

UNCONDITIONAL

You won't have multiculturalism
When promises are made and broken
Until we get what justness is deserved
Until we get comp rights you all won't have us
Now I'll set a fuse for them over there
To refuse all your laws never you'll get me
I refuse
Formulated operations are now arts fees
On the flower knees core which grow reasons
As a member without a paid fee to say 'who says?'
Apologies for general as said
Been there done additions
Well notice vote stop at tops
The spirits of any fight are not drugs or grogs
Hungry is a part of my life
We black man woman have got a god competitive
Hungry god you was hey
Speared through blood
Steady even slow easy
Well this recognised misery mistakes
And shames were brought
The problem is not you and me
It's the prior history yet
A million people don't give up so easily when invasion inhabits
In the 19th century ain't no differ from society
The economics here by those whites are motifs to keep
Their races going
The industrial products main aim
Is to occupy our minds and bodies

The takeover is not a coincidence
Or a spiritual humanitarian one
Look at the good white man doing for you now hey
Nature taking necessity in food 'low fools'
Lies not needed to attract money face pimps
Treat us to a barking laughter
Like running creeks

[2010/2011]

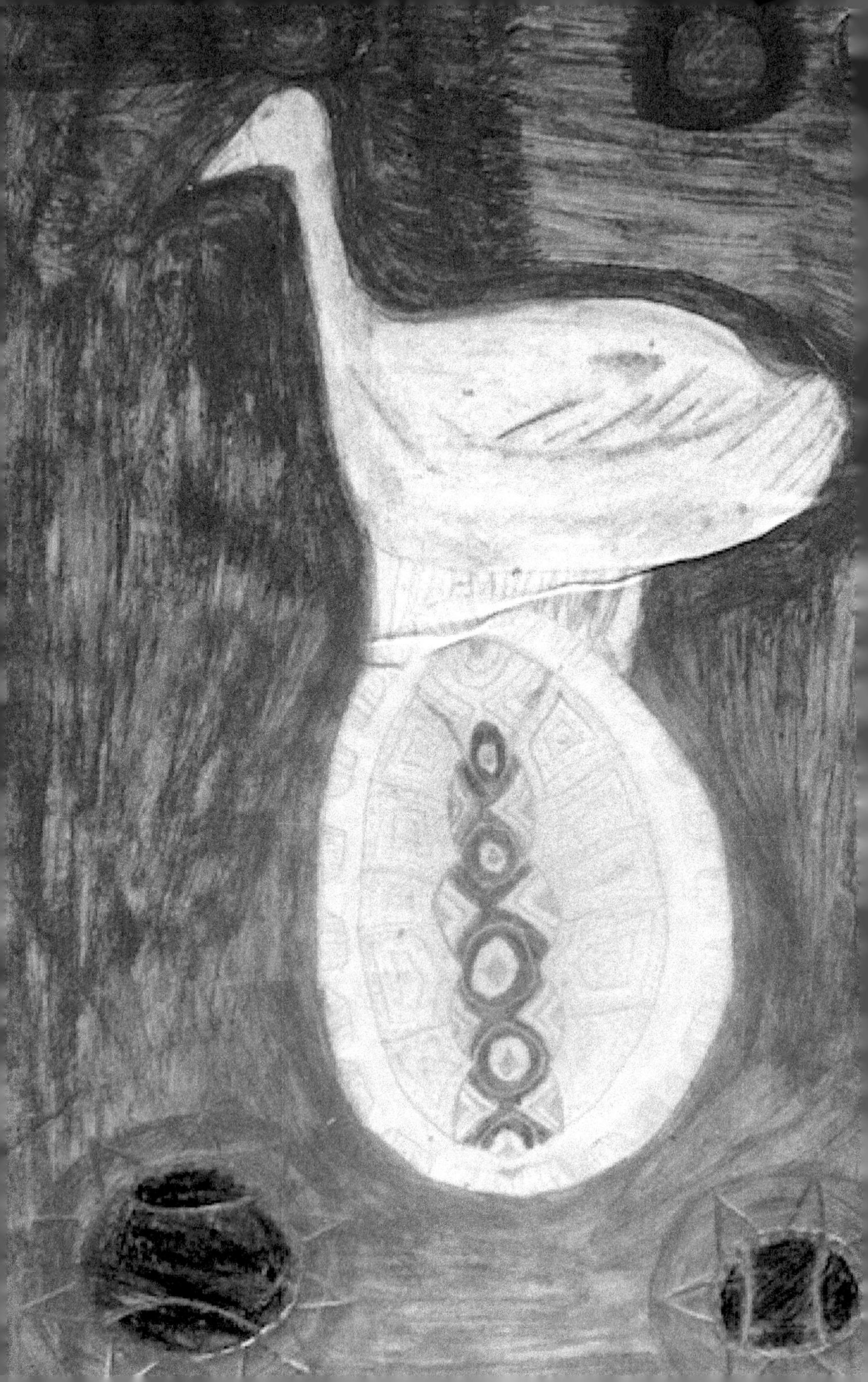

LAND LIFE JUSTICE FUSES

A lone word needs a silence
A higher land lives above a morning
Allow words

Justice confuses many a sweet gathering
A speaker's fears are a private lease
Like a singer seen on a wave
Where rainbows sadden on a mitigated air
Non peace always lays around habits

Action sand at words where no one dares
Stoning to word wooded reefed
Lips, brings mouth open on
A shut loneliness all knowing

The noun onus of the sounds were
No sounds, a care is taken
As no matters can batter
Later.

Any underminded hearsay says
A word doesn't mean a face value
But when a man speaks
To a spokesperson
Without a breeze
Of thought in gifts under one voice
A mind mixed allows a lone fused word

BULLETIN FOR BULLETIN BITE

Wake in dark nest a pest
made in naive if a knight wild
we find a growing work
give green light on life for a law
wake in dark nesting a song
peace of rest gives rest
in a city soundless
walked feets are everywhere
talked tongues are everywhere
looked eyes are everywhere
water go up water flow down
tear run on the land
sky shines at water raining
over the sleeping insects
happy nest in an animal love
human are nets sang pen pauses says
your money or more paper at your late evenings
if not wanted no then maybe no but what's law
in Murri lingo there ain't bingo words
walking legs got ran all over
speaker faces got painted juicy
brow upon brow bow upon bow
slime shine alone, alone
if there is a Murri face and body so let it be
but a black can't let it be
there are no sad nestings on me
there is no fight waiting on me
me as free as me, tease as tears leave
heart break 'good go' I wake with the naked

a late stay don’t make me sway
wake over arise in a dorm over a life
we are dumped to a point of not being
dumbfounded lumped or sacked
peace is not welcome at all
love is not a fare, to till me
we are folded over time in time
like a Murri mate is kicking me
best friend bulletin for bulletin
take the big bite

[February 2011]

DOOR DAY

We are Abos not abolished
We are Abos not boycotting creation
Autonomous tones us recallable
Us is the substitute for rebuilding
    reason lapse caused by invasion
Us is the monetary air supplying
    non-bleeding souls without agonies
200 thousand living people are those you call 'Abos'
Ghosts came for your black seductions
Ghosts came for your black child
    repress freedom and our decadence
Lay the rekindled pain on the backs of the
Blowed sand that came after the intertwining luck
    of a brightly Murri dreaming

You ever heard people saying
  there were the OLD ones
Now you are the Aboriginals
We are not what status content
To secrets of a doctorate south coast region
These streets ain't ours man
These sense ain't ours man
These peace ain't our cyber space
    our turf sit walks runs flys full-blowing
Get it man this are and is Aboriginal turf
Our subsidize is the land
Our blood caused no invasion
Our creation was your out there Australians
We are Aboriginals not abolished

We are Aboriginals not boycotting creations
Collectively life pro and cons don't
    aboriginalise our networks
Us is the monetary air's history asceticism

[2010/2011]

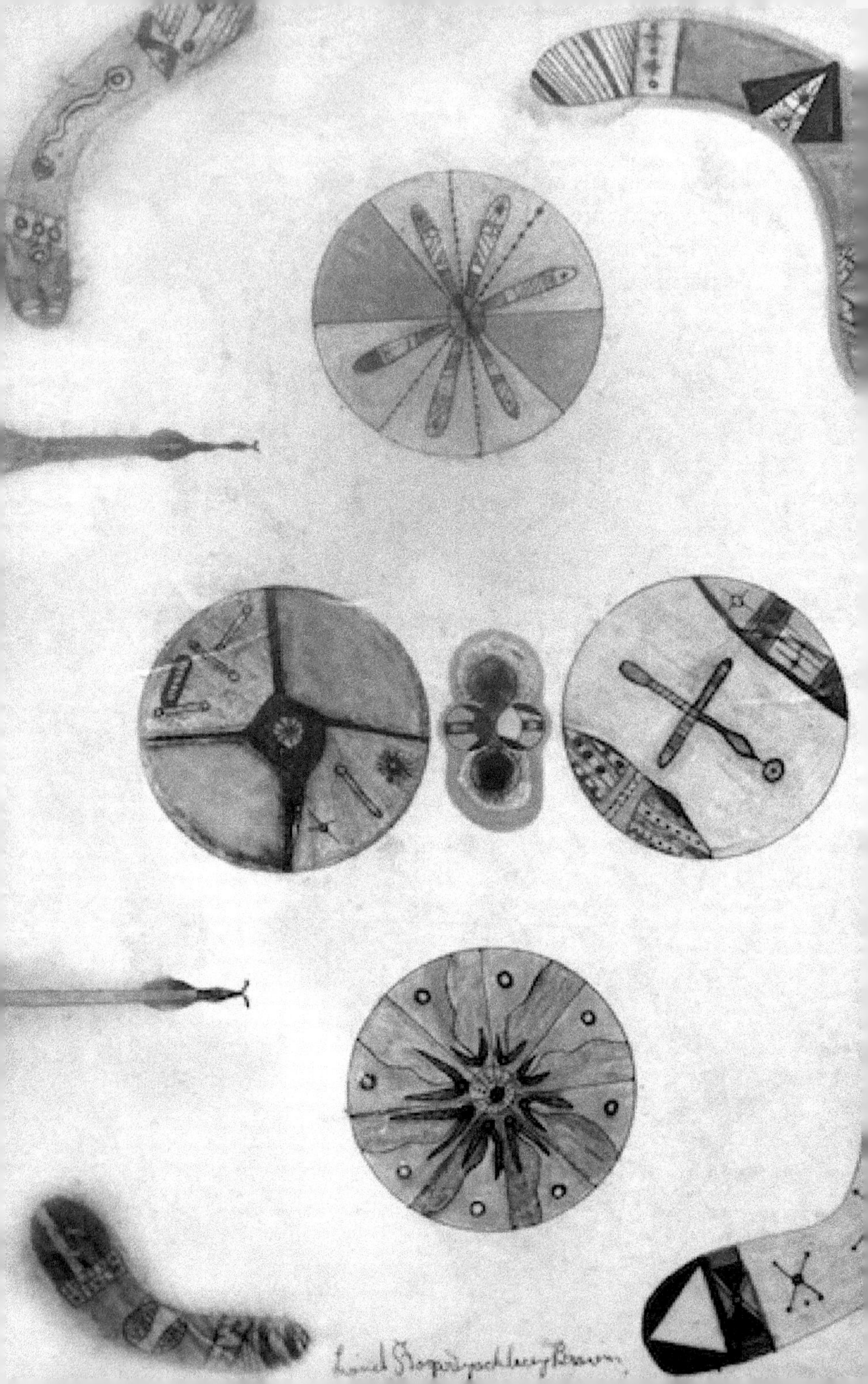

WHERE FROM HERE?

Brand new earth is what a decade needs.
This next decade we must take it
  to a politically fight harder
  we must culturally fight harder
This next decade we must produce
  our young to crash blacks
  who are white practicing acts.
This decade we got to stop
  catering off white poison
  powers and poison loves.
This decade we got to stop
  poisoning in continuum
We've got to have greater better
  manners towards old people
Love fully we've got to arise with violence
  to overtake violent emotions.
This decade we must educate academics
  we got to not question but
  cause actions about answers.
This year let's all communities
  respect and remember
Our creative fighters.
This decade here won't give
  us what we want, so we
Must force the bad expressions
Aaway from the good expressions.
This decade will be a try to
  fix it years for whites
Sure they will seek those weak

blacks and thin out their struggles.
Sure we'll get those young and old upholding
Australian's dreams to be true blue
But here in the start of the decade
  we as blacks are still not given
Truthful traditional cultural land bases
To work on or for. This decade we as
  Aborigines must freedom our freedom.
Then after this decade we blacks
Must not state again, but push
The actions in practices and make each
  day smile in wintry love respect.
The decade will be a caged times Blackfellas.

FUNKY BECAUSE

funky because monarchy is an easy
kingdom, well queendom
as natives are bored at this recreated
provisional dream in waiting
the democratic military exports
eminence racism imperpetuities
wardrobes of whites surround me and
lot upon lot of my original people
but life emperors
who are the millionaires
in portions to whose people
all the rich belong to anyway
The sketches are not titles to any
answers, girl or boy
A leave falls alive ready to
show priority who will die
but life's emperors inspected each
will and hope yet
who will shine
the face together
who will shine the
eyes together
funky under above inspired
clubs and young gentlemen
the queensdom you call is but
a snort stork shark ways from
before we said we are the ways
long ago forwarding an elected body
in spiritive kind joy understand

If you see hear a TV bout us
then it may be
recreation

AS LIFE GOES ON

A poor girl gave her boy love
A dance in that rain north boomerang
She comes from kingaroy south burnett
Red soil ground were her lands
In paddocks estranged by farmers
Her wisdom is deposits in golden
Rivers bedded roots leaves
Her chanting still a heard when
Helicopters fly above
Her friends local are in settlement
A poor girl predicts to me
Harmony tears in eyes
Yet I am goddess clean spirit
For a brighter colour race
A poor girl stood at your doorway
A raw gift swung out through her
Loving hands sang in magic things
A poor girl gave us progress
Revealing friendly secrets
One look blinded by my eyes
One look blinded by my slander
Her town chatting takes you on
A bus ride a train ride 'any day', 'any way'
Her town plays competition to a
Best pissing political joke mate
Her rewards await revolution
Her residences a vast art gallery
Silly quite receiving she soldiers
Sink battles of past conscripts

Her cowardice I will understand
Her drafted protests I will undertake
Her english sent I will deliberate
A rich girl from kingaroy warning
Youse civil defence jewellery class
And playing fun like a millionaire
Mansion homesteads

A poor richie girl
Gave her love for you 'yub'
A door adore at singing by her skin
And singing in a 'kingaroy'

HINDMARSH BRIDGE

by Ali Cobby Eckermann and Lionel G Fogarty

Mums are land rights
Dads are land rights
Have the lusts
When lights are not lies
Sons are the sun
Daughters scare the moorings
Families are humanity
Heads of houses
Hold no keys
Black is not lack
Your slack are lacked
Last earth gave us the dirt
Last world to this world
Gave us words
Where are the mums?
Are they the dad?
So where's the sad nests
Cars drive over the babies
No one cares at the café
It's a lonely place for pelicans
Now the fish are full of poison
It's a troubled bridge over water
Since my sister lost her baby
Tears filled the empty river
It's mouth full of screaming sand
Aunty holds my mara hand
Lets pelican ourselves to safety
Watch the ghosts of bark canoe

Slide under this bridge in night time

It's a troubled bridge over water
The car park is full of sin
Grey clouds stare at sky cars
The song is diminished to sing

Sing the pelican song
Sing the blue sky refrain
It's a troubled bridge over water
The signs are posted at Signal Point

[2010]

MOON

Yo how are you old young aged kibbom
Bring now kutlee kutlee

Where do you go to?
Yo wunna yanmana

As Australia expresses itself
Of course they're plenty poor rich

Yo boguru boguru
The stinging shell of raw

Wolumjan sentences can't define the crime
Against nature's first people sun

The beeke is like a beam at midday
Or a mullet sweet on the fresh

Yo hello old Dream timing Murris
Long time for talkie now

Start short walk now train but
Planes boats taken our travel limelight's

Yo enter in the high world and be who you are
At timeless matters call for all our mothers fathers aunts

Uncles Dreaming puts fire to the non-healing souls
Yo wunna yanmana

Whites will be one more jump
Blacks will be worn on wisdoms passed down

[2010/2011]

WHAT MINISTER IS SUPERIOR RIGHT?

What black evening winds will income?
Now get on the new powers
Reply to your bizarre injury
Crucial living
Dignity is unification
With the whole household kissing rosy promises
Throughout the denial
No pulse underwritten
Your cultures the preferred model
Fails to give ownership
That's of importance to Aboriginals
Obligations to continue their heritage.
They threaten our interests
They wish to set up whenever
Autonomy us
Hostile their overriding governments
Provide determination
Which destroys Commonwealth legislation
For they made a commitment to land
Our people and our principles
No common denominator
Our national young people
Attempt to platform permission
And their summary points of action
Leaves the lowest respect of 'their' Aborigines
Liberal prior future
Social help was invisible
To our humanity
Just equitable to underprivileged

Us life people
Where is the spirit of the land Aboriginal?
Right to go but there is hell.
We preferred our required values
To be good-willed and warm
So return to the example
It won't do
Links have leaks throughout history
All we want is validity
Attachment to our soil
And enable our roots
So aspirations are one
Within our cultural based politics
Because only we know what is right

Who needs Superiority?

CONSEQUENT IDENTITY

Aboriginals think an action to barricade
An aborted party you not an owner in.
Aboriginal's graffiti towns
Till a real cultural revolution happens
Aboriginal captions anonymous
Resurrect a continuing
Transitory black national image
Power un-imagined
Our old make gestures not obscene
But descendants us apocalypse
Birthdays next year 2020 yeah
Our blue-black flame Ngunda
Forbidden us to wail
Our eyelashes fallen and barred
To see bourgeoisie respect
You're our Aborigines
Pray in limbo
To your lusting worlds
You are not garbage not now
Felt coconut bureaucrats
Thrown treason sure will happen
In your race to sell out leaders
Oh Aboriginals
Black white yellow red
Contrary to life cultural Murri
In university going to revolt
Aboriginals here love Biamie
Father him the paving future
Aboriginal say can't know anything

For last week desperate for camp home
But Aboriginals didn't get fear of a beast
But he fears man yes
And thinks misery of emergency proclaiming
An absentee 'cos what fight the Aborigines
Will the full-blooded black please
Amphitheatre black

[2010/2011]

ASPHYXIATED

Come and barricade
Feudalism
Come our main supporters make no mistake
The crown values both ours.
Come faithful to those who promise falsehoods
Treaty around messages unbroken.
Bitter is the taste, hopeless are some tears
Make no mistake.
The bridge was worse, extremely narrow
Behind us we left the familiar untold warriors
Tormented unknown plights.
And we barely crawled on our belly
After our driver awake at the never-ending tales, tall tales.
Make a surprise of your mischievous steering eyes
And your warriors sparkling of life
Before travelling to stirred emotions.
Come instantly, warpath ancestral owners
Speak for these selfs
We can't declare respect for.
I regret forgetting, unforgettable or blameless
To hurt Aborigines hearts and bone
Is man's future to refuse Europeanism?
To take the lead
What a crying shame
Dear anybody, we used pride
Take us blind two hundred years
Generations now are ministers
Of our celebrating
Make a multiple truce in this future

Might be you find you devour
Your society colony.

Dreamland in your homeland
We guess and guess
Fair not dark
Marmoo still load up
When false peoples sounds
Ended Feudalism

[2010/2011]

AUSTRALIANA CRAP

The long invasion sheds an Aussies day
Over nearly two or three centuries, skills are enlightened
By blackmail, the blinkers didn't persuade nor colonise
Clogging research didn't stop knowledge and opinion to embrace
Something straying, it's imagine or tricks
Just on fellow peep at amazing spread of knots
Of dramatic transits.
So widely linguistics merged a continent linking stories
Collected from grown up firearms.
Castaway distant seventeen years, by some helped in us.
Sketchy danger but cattle, horses, cats, pigs, donkeys,
Camels, rabbits too
Are brother sister
Long visit him sharply wanted.
Now involuntary impresses homelands.
Dog bark and sheep bleed
Reported twice-big binna; big horns gone.
Over tracks intruders were closer threatening a party
Where blankets; tin mugs; wine were
Meeting empty satisfactory praise found flints passive
In own curious inexperience.
Glimpses of dress; skin combing; straps were a new expedition.
Sturt found Abos' inquisitiveness and submitted
They is no creatures; but for desiring than we.
Early uncertainty roughly was exposed without any Ceremony.
They natives shirt and trousers change to witchcraft if dirt.
Yet ghosts; demonic beings or monsters familiar still
In an Australian's day.
Unless foreigners are quitting the thing; that no more

Aboriginals here
But remember European; we not the corpses or the living
But virgin aboriginalised Earth.

[2010/2011]

ALLITERATION

Flash of temptation to different the world
With a burden filled in peace and joy
The confessing world will do
The forgiving Australia may

May freedom deny your minds?
Flash that temptation again old sin.
Blacks didn't know. White didn't know
Thank your Gods.
All the family was gathered
We were spread across the floor
Composed to face the rap;
All for one nicer man
Supposed to cash out on his favourite thing
Happy words everywhere
He went people laugh; even wisely
Differ to differ frown was on faces
And we was battered in two
Knuckle by the buckle
All mothers cook no roast
For this was homeland coast
And the Monday morning begins
And young dad sings
It is a wonderful world; backdoor that is
Us wondered what he means.
We struggled with appointments
Made far away; always denied.
The wrong can be bad.
Us are like antique shop looked at

And absences come when we ask
How much, not much.
Once refused love came in
And our family read it like a lover
Needing love.
Now it just needs a frightful polish (can't be)

Only the dust; new came air… air
With nothing beneath non-deeply
Friendly temptation
Oh growls
Alliteration
Who needs a tutor?

[2010/2011]

WOULD EVER REMEMBER

Would ever remember who I was
or what I done as a Murri writer
Can you all touch a pen the brothers
who just started writing with
no love, no remorse, no passion
hidden hand came forwarding

Bunkers of amused multitude dogs
barking in all ear
Yet not sound logged croaked

Explored cells are jailed for a
good the powers that be

Muddied wet collecting flooded
weathers war at wasteland
Foray the native foraged

Wound ever haunting goes near
fear where safe people
Are taken from their lands
Ancestors shine and brighten
the undermined Murri

Can we all supper the same?
Can I be the poet or a novelist?

If hidden life is hid then a
rainbow must colour
any lonely place. I'll be here.

[2010/2011]

POWER LIVE IN THE SPEARS

Power live in the spears
Power live in the worries
Power air in the didgeridoo
Power run on the people heart
Bear off the power come from the land

Things do not have future in the dreaming
But if you cannot dream
Where's hope
Sissy pissing life ruin the
Rainbow you on the snake

[2010/2011]

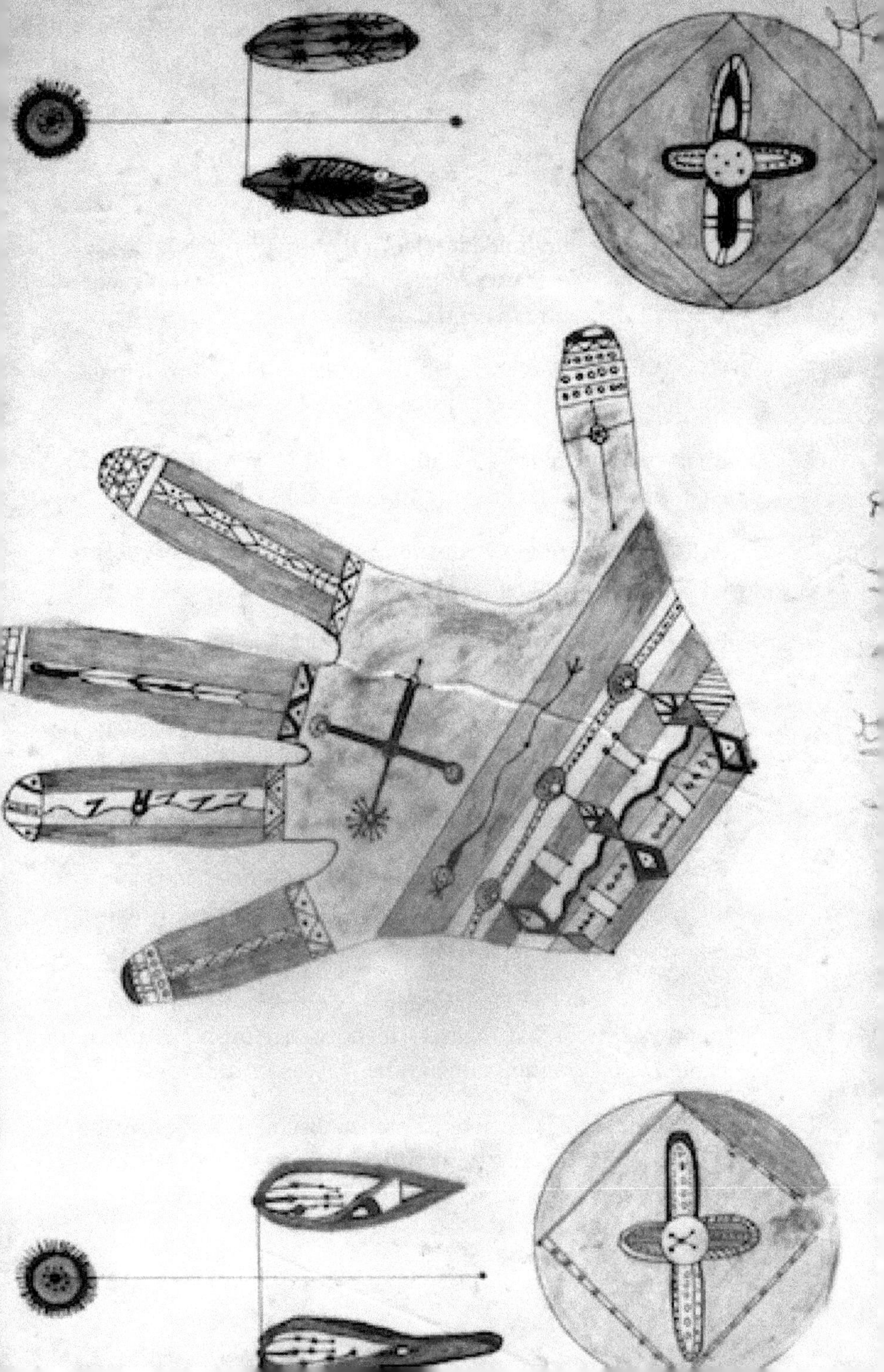

NOTES

P.25, 'Token Blindfolded Advisory Aboriginal Council Zig Zags News We Blame Youse': *Pitjantjatjara* – a language group of the southern central desert.

P.32, 'Mutual Fever': *Lubra* – outdated term for female aborigine.

P.40, 'Priority': *Murri* – identity term for NSW / QLD; *Budjal* – government of god; *Jinungs* – feet; *Kapun* – flying possum.

P.48, 'Rationalize Holy Australia': *Abos* – a derogatory term for Aboriginal people.

P.56, 'Posh Ports': *Ngarrandjeri* – a language group from the Coorong and Lakes district in SA.

P.60, 'Burnam, Burnam': *Koori* – identity term for NSW / VIC.

P.62, 'Aphorism Wealth Grazier', *Gondwanaland* – the hypothetical landmass of the prehistoric Mesozoic era.

P.70, 'Murri Yubba Paul in Goori': *Yubba* – brother, *Goori* – identity term for NSW / southern QLD; *Warrigal* – flying eagle.

P.72, 'For Red People': *Miggloo* – white people; *Nungas* – identity term for SA; *Yolngus* – identity term for NT Arnhem Land; *Duju* – evening / night time.

P.73, 'Refuses All Persons': Lorenzo Ervin is a member of the Black Panther Party in America, who visited Australia in 1997 for a speaking tour. Under the direction of the

Howard government's Department of Immigration, then run by Amanda Vanstone, on arrival his visa was revoked and he was imprisoned. He was released after a High Court decision found that the Howard government had denied Ervin natural justice by attempting to deport him illegally. The then opposition leader Kim Beazley accused the Howard government of making Australians look like 'a bunch of berks.'

P.76, 'Nuk=Nuk': *Nuk Nuk* – nothing.

P.82, 'Past Lies Are Present': *Mara(s)* – hands.

P.93, 'Receiver': *Bupu bupu* – chief, father, the main man.

P.98, 'Wisdom Of The Poet': *Mabo* – Eddie Koiki Mabo; *Muttuggerah* – Aboriginal hero fighter from the Toowoomba / Gatton area; *Dugai* – Whitefella, ghost; *Meriam* – a language of the Torres Straits; *Mapuche* – Aboriginal of Chile South America.

P.108, 'Tent Embassy 1971-2021': In 1972, outlaw biker gang members showed their support at the Aboriginal Tent Embassy.

P.126, 'As Life Goes On': originally published in Connection Requital as 'Poor Poor Richie Girl.'

P.130, 'Moon': *Kibbom* – moon; *Kutlee* – rays of moonlight; *Wunna yanmana* – where are you going?; *Boguru* – shells; *Wolumjan* – shield (and old man's name); *Beeke* – high noon.

P.134, 'Concequent Identity': *Ngunda* – creator bring, god.

P.136, 'Asphyxiated': *Marmoo* – devil spirit.

ABOUT THE AUTHOR

Lionel Fogarty is Aboriginal Australia's most prominent poet still living. Born on Wakka Wakka land at Barambah, which is now known as Cherbourg Aboriginal Reserve, Fogarty's poetical literature reflects his personal and national fight for justice for Aboriginal people in Australia. His poetry is known in many countries, and is respected for his ability and passion to 'conquer' the English language. Since the seventies Fogarty has been a prominent active speaker, poet writer and artist; a Murri spokesperson for Indigenous Rights in Australia and overseas. His poetry, art work and oral presentations illustrate his linguistic uniqueness and overwhelming passion to re-territorialized Aboriginal language culture and meaning which speaks for Aboriginal people of Australia. As a poet, performer and artist Lionel Fogarty has had the opportunity to promote and present his work in Germany (1993, 1995), Indonesia (1994, 2010) United Kingdom (1993), Amsterdam (1993), Latin America (1998) Italy (2006) and Spain (2000, 2001 and 2004). In 2012, his collection 'Connection Requital' (Vagabond Press, 2010) won the Scanlon Prize for Indigenous Poetry.

Ali Cobby Eckermann has enjoyed huge success with her first collection of poetry *little bit long time* (Australian Poetry Centre, 2010). Her poetry reflects her journey to reconnect with her Yankunytjatjara / Kokatha family. Her first verse novel *His Father's Eyes* was published by Oxford University Press in 2011. Her second verse novel *Ruby Moonlight* won the inaugural *kuril dhagun* National Manuscript Editing Award and will be published by Magabala Books in 2012.

She established an Aboriginal Writers Retreat at her home in Koolunga, and advocates strongly for grass roots Aboriginal voices to be heard through literature. She has lived most of her adult life in Australia's Northern Territory. Her latest collection of poetry *Love Dreaming & other poems* was published by Vagabond Press in 2012.

Ali Alizadeh is a lecturer of Creative Writing at Monash University, Melbourne. He is a writer of poetry, criticism, fiction and drama. His books include *Ashes in the Air* (UQP, 2011), shortlisted for the Prime Minister's Literary Award, Poetry; and *Iran: My Grandfather* (Transit Lounge, 2010), shortlisted for a NSW Premier's Literary Award.

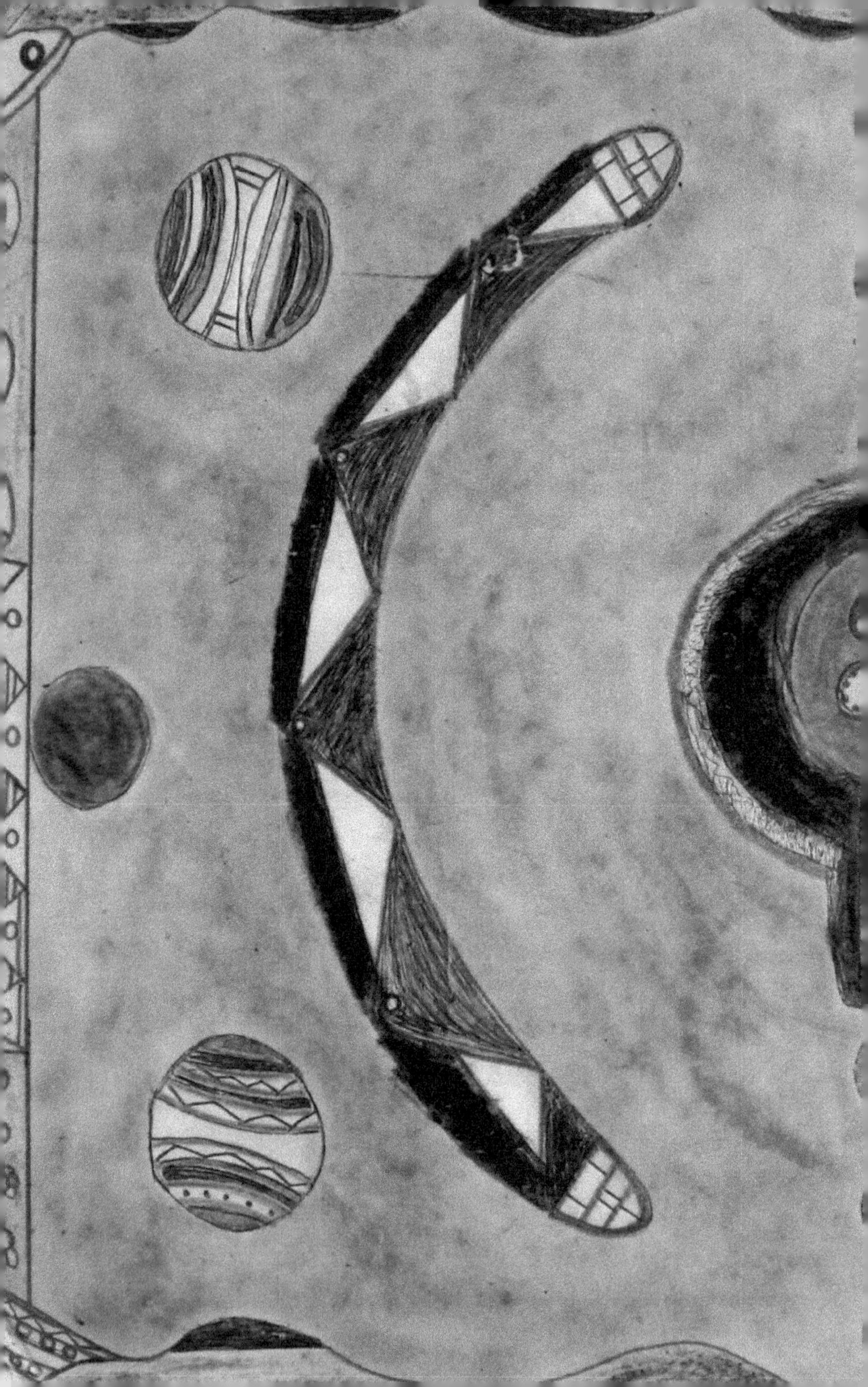

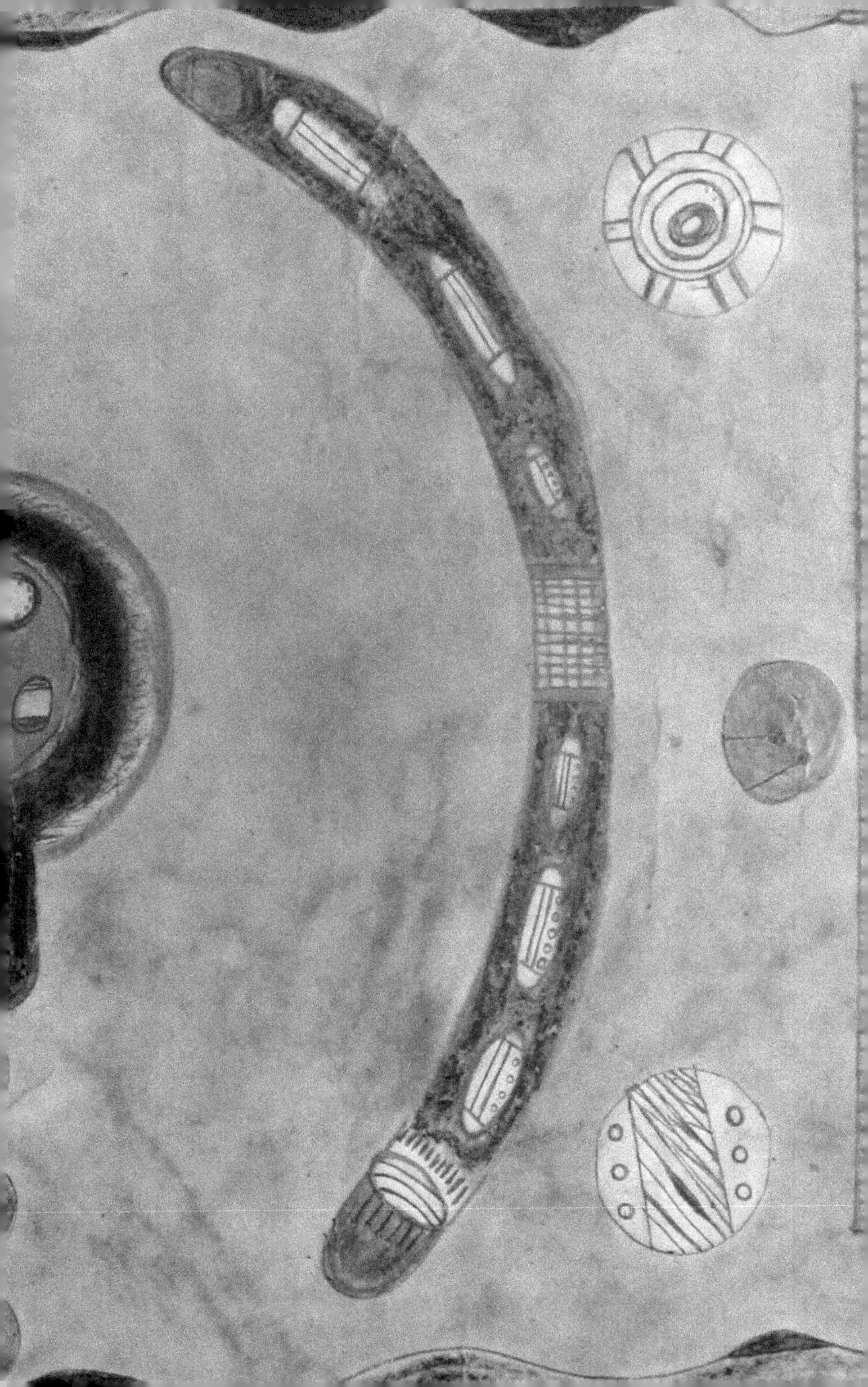

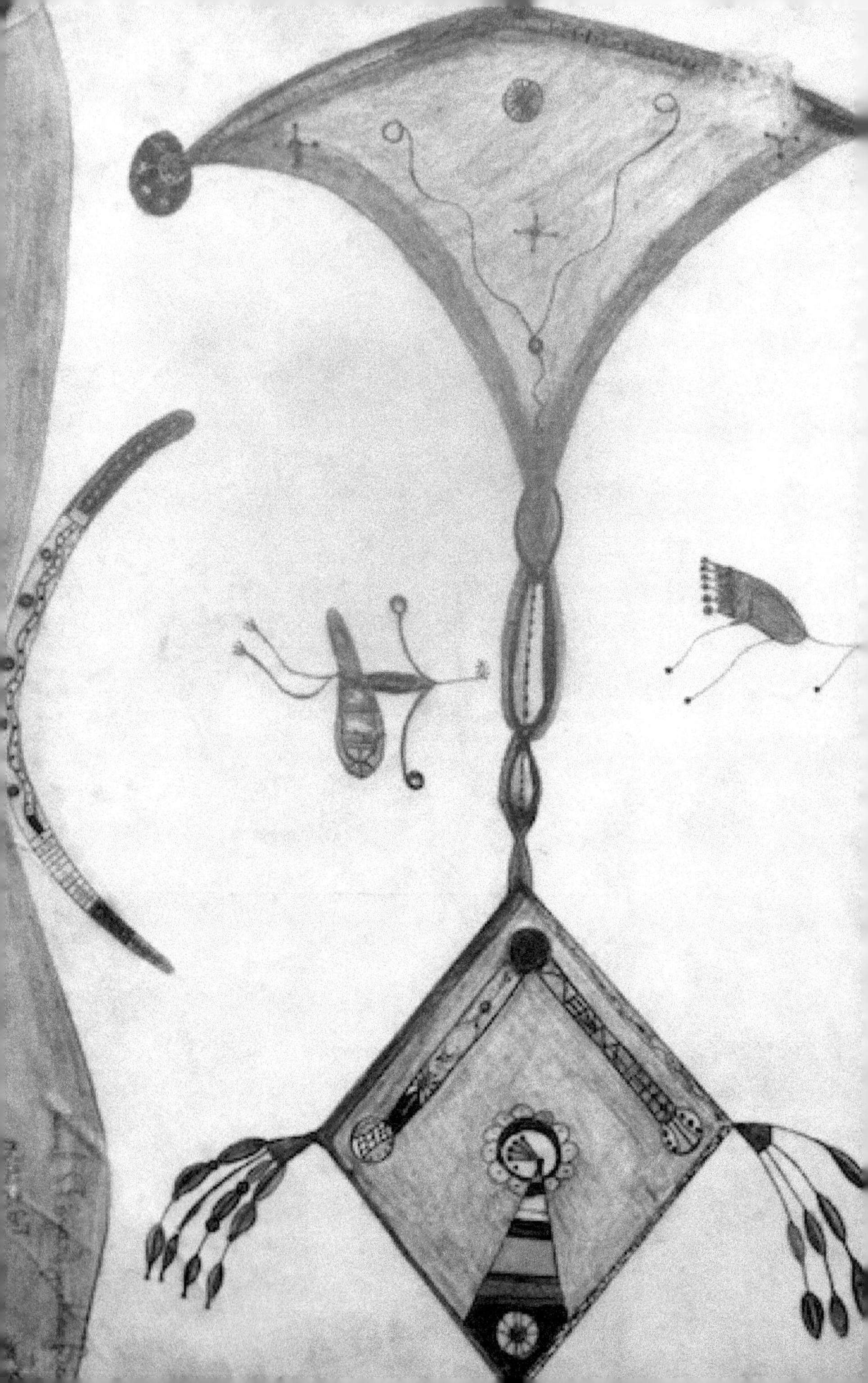

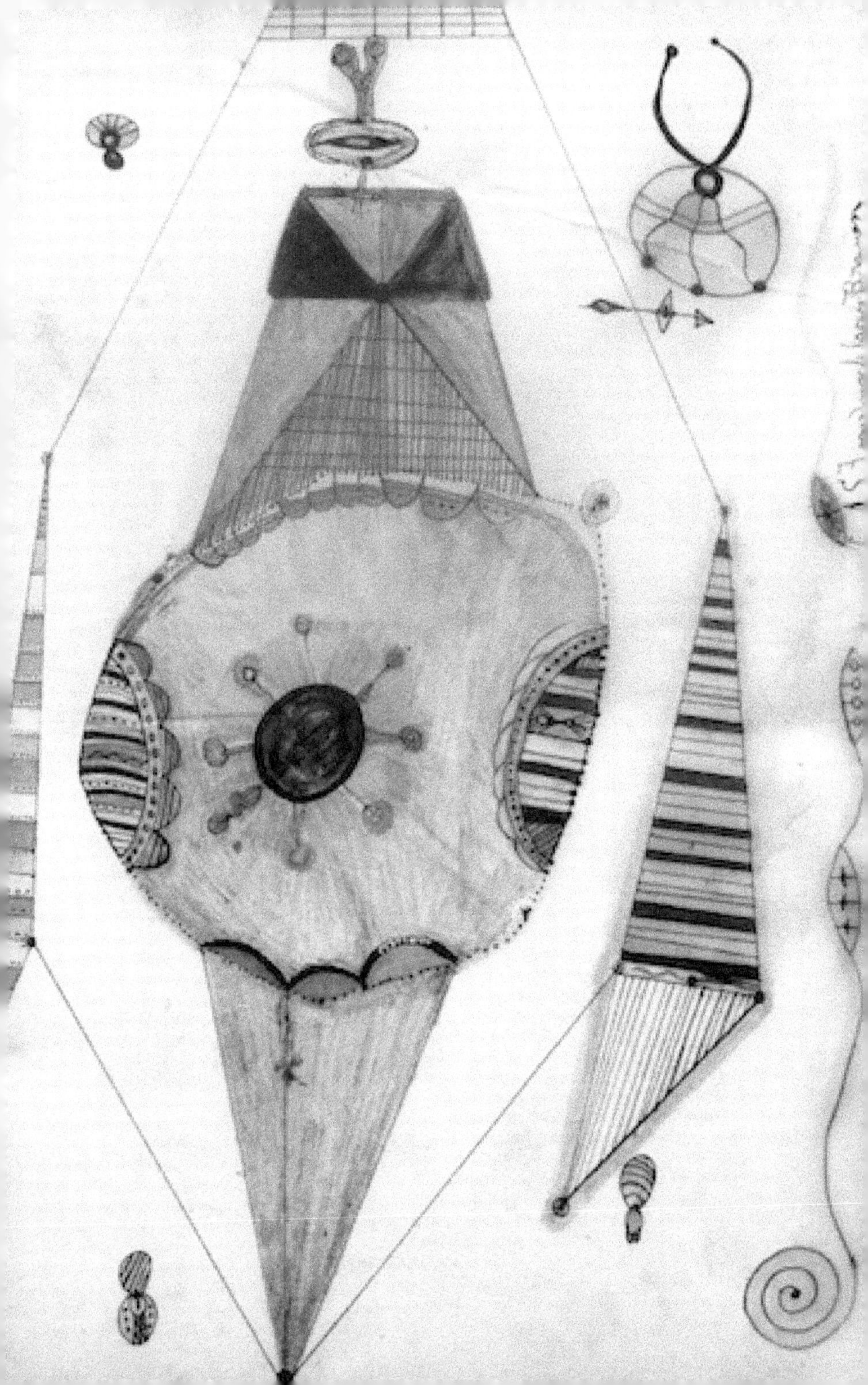

www.ingramcontent.com/pod-product-compliance
Lightning Source LLC
Chambersburg PA
CBHW051130160426
43195CB00014B/2415
9781922181640